MAKING A DIFFERENCE

Reflections on life, leadership and politics

To Elissa!
Best wishes,
Peter Beattie
28.6.05

MAKING A DIFFERENCE

Reflections on life, leadership and politics

PETER BEATTIE

WITH ANGELO LOUKAKIS

HarperCollins*Publishers*

HarperCollinsPublishers

First published in Australia in 2005
by HarperCollinsPublishers Pty Limited
ABN 36 009 913 517
A member of the HarperCollinsPublishers (Australia) Pty Limited Group
www.harpercollins.com.au

Peter Beattie acknowledges the help of Angelo Loukakis
in the writing of this book.

HarperCollinsPublishers
25 Ryde Road, Pymble, Sydney, NSW 2073, Australia
31 View Road, Glenfield, Auckland 10, New Zealand
77–85 Fulham Palace Road, London, W6 8JB, United Kingdom
2 Bloor Street East, 20th floor, Toronto, Ontario M4W 1A8, Canada
10 East 53rd Street, New York NY 10022, USA

National Library of Australia Cataloguing-in-Publication data:

Beattie, Peter.
 Making a difference: reflections on life, leadership and politics.
 Includes index.
 ISBN 0 7322 7399 4.
 1. Beattie, Peter, 1952– . 2. Australian Labor Party –
 Biography. 3. Premiers – Queensland – Biography.
 4. Queensland – Politics and government – 1976–1990.
 5. Queensland – Politics and government – 1990– .
 I. Title.
352.23092

Cover design by Natalie Winter, HarperCollins Design Studio
Front cover photograph by Vincent Long
Back cover photographs (clockwise): a young Peter Beattie in Atherton; with New Zealand
Prime Minister Helen Clark; with Heather Beattie in 1987; with brothers and sisters, 1956;
with Dr Shaikh Sultan bin Khalifa Al Nahyan in the United Arab Emirates, 2003; Peter
Beattie's mother, Edna Beattie; addressing the South Carolina Legislature; (clockwise) Larissa,
Heather, Matthew and Denis Beattie; receiving an Honorary Doctorate of Science, with (left
to right) Arthur Beattie, Judy Beattie, Joan Dowling, Anthony Dowling, Lynette Usher and
Bill Beattie; Heather and Peter Beattie; with a Papua New Guinean war veteran, 2002; with
the former President of China Jiang Zemin; with Queen Elizabeth II; with then Governor of
Texas, George W. Bush, 1999; President of St John's College, 1974.
Internal design by HarperCollins Design Studio
Typeset in 12 on 19pt Minion by Kirby Jones
Printed and bound in Australia by Griffin Press on 79gsm Bulky Paperback White

5 4 3 2 1   05 06 07 08

'A state without the means of some change is without the means of its conservation.'

EDMUND BURKE

'The Labour Party is a moral crusade or it is nothing.'

HAROLD WILSON, BRITISH PRIME MINISTER, 1964

CONTENTS

PROLOGUE

When I was approached to write a 'memoir' some time back, I had misgivings. Though sports stars happily write memoirs in their twenties, vanity suggested I wasn't old enough, even at fifty and counting. The fact that I am still active in political life brings constraints, and not just in defamation law. I am mindful of the gloss some of my contemporaries have applied to their own efforts in this area, and also that books by politicians are often greeted with scepticism or plain cynicism.

But then, with prompting from my 'amanuensis', Angelo Loukakis, I thought of the upside. I could take the opportunity to try to analyse where I have come from and where I am headed, both in politics and in my personal life; I could try to be cold-eyed about my achievements and failures generally, find the measure of what mattered in my life and in the life of my political party, and try to signpost some ways forward.

Once underway, however, I realised that I would not be able to effectively do these things without telling a couple of other stories as I went along. I am a Queenslander. My fortunes have been bound up in those of the state I call home. And my personal development has been tied in with the growth and change of the Australian Labor Party, the political party I have had the privilege to lead in Queensland. The Party and the state are much bigger than me and, in the end, matter more than I do. In any account I might write, I would want to do them justice and give them their proper place. So this is not a 'tell all' — mine cannot be that kind of memoir, for what I hope are understandable reasons. Perhaps what follows in this book are not so much memoirs as a series of reflections.

What has evolved is a narrative set out in three parts. The first, 'Early Lessons', pretty much covers the things that mattered to me in early life and helped shape the person I became. The second part, 'Up Through the Ranks', tracks my political career. In the third part, 'Visions and Values', I talk about the messages I draw from the first two parts and talk about what I hope for in the futures of my society, my family and myself.

This is my story and these are my thoughts; I am happy to leave judgments to the reader and to history.

Part I

EARLY LESSONS

I t's an interesting challenge, trying to figure out what has shaped you as a person. Pitfalls abound. Do you have all the information needed and is it correct? How well do you really know yourself and is that how others see you? How much are you a product of nature as against nurture? Maybe it's not so much the brave as the foolish who would even take on such a task.

As for being my own biographer, I'm not convinced I'm the best person for the job. But I do see some connections between my origins and where I am today. I hope that my attempt to describe these might be of interest or even use to others.

An older Australia cradled me, one which has largely disappeared. Maybe the broad outline of that Australia is visible, so too some of the better values, but certainly it has disappeared in the details. Daily life when I was a youngster back in the '50s was a very different thing to daily life as children and adolescents experience it in the early part of the twenty-first century. But we all know about the rapid changes in things like travel and electronic communications, the explosion in entertainment choices.

Life is more comfortable today in the provision of material goods and services. But in my view, there have been losses as well as gains. People look at the world so differently now, and it can seem less kind than the one I grew up in. Still — with the important provisos of a stable home with someone who loves you, and a culture that doesn't teach envy or resentment — the world can still feel like a place of possibilities. That was how it was for many of us in that economically poorer Australia following World War II.

Casual observers of our lives in Atherton, a small rural town in far north Queensland, might have seen a bum-out-of-the-pants existence, one constrained by poverty and lacking in opportunity; some of us could see differently. In important ways, ours was a rich community. It encompassed many cultural backgrounds; a visible Indigenous component let you know that Australia wasn't solely a white man's world; there were decent — if by today's standards under-resourced — schools. Among the staff were often good, dedicated teachers who were interested in the welfare and futures of their students. A high value was placed on education — by the humble as well as the teachers and the achievers. There were spaces where you could kick a ball around and plenty of grounds for organised sports; there was reasonably full employment, even for labouring men and women. Not for a minute am I suggesting that everyone coming from that environment went on to personal success and contentment. But everyone had at least some chance in life. The rest, as they would say, was up to you.

What message can I draw from my own start in life? I would address parents, especially people of my generation, the much-maligned 'baby-boomers'. Instil hope, not fear or despair, into your kids; teach them the importance of thrift and enjoying the small pleasures of life. Help them understand what really counts, that it's not having the most fashionable clothes or the latest electronic gadgetry. Above all, try to impress on them that personal satisfaction springs from honest effort, and from staying connected with other people and involved to whatever extent possible in their wellbeing.

EARLY LIFE

First memories

Mum and Dad, Edna and Arthur Beattie, were living in Condobolin in western New South Wales when I was born. Dad was managing a property there called 'Roma'. The seventh and last child of the family, I was born on 18 November 1952, and my parents christened me Peter Douglas Beattie. I was born in Sydney because my mother needed specialist medical care. Mum had serious heart problems and she died before I turned five.

In our age of equality it is difficult to argue that mothers are more important than fathers. But for young children they are. Sadly, I have precious few memories of my mother. Qualities of warmth and kindness are what come to my mind in relation to Mum. One of my few images is of running from the old school bus into her outstretched arms. What I'd been doing on the bus that day, as I wasn't yet attending school, I don't recall.

My sisters tell me Mum went out of her way to spend time talking to me, cuddling and encouraging me — knowing how unwell she was. When she died, I was simply told she had gone away. I knew something was horribly wrong. I knew she wouldn't go without me. Eventually I found out the truth. My life had been turned upside down.

I missed my mother's warmth and her support. My sisters and brothers were a great comfort, but the fact was we had all lost our mother.

A family dispersed

Dad was suddenly alone with six young children — David, one of my brothers, had died in 1956, at the age of eight. It wasn't do-able. So our family was split up; we were sent in all different directions.

Edna, the eldest, stayed in Condobolin and is there to this day. She married a wonderful man by the name of Joe Kiss, a Hungarian who fled after the uprising and the subsequent Soviet invasion of 1956. Never once since then has he set foot back in Hungary. My next sister, Lyn, went to Brisbane to live with Mum's sister, Aunty Norrie. Joan went to Sydney to live with Mum's other sister, Aunty Vena. That left Dad and us boys — Arthur, Bill and me. For a while we lived in Londonderry, on the outskirts of Sydney. It didn't work out. Dad lost too much money gambling on the races. Arthur was sent off to live with my grandmother, Annie Esbensen, our Nana, in

Atherton, a small farming town in far north Queensland. He was only there for a short time before moving on to Goroka in Papua New Guinea. Bill and Dad would eventually shift to Orange in NSW, and there Dad later remarried. But before their move to Orange it was agreed that, because I was the youngest, I should also go and live with Nana.

Travelling alone

Aged just seven, I made that long journey on my own. Dad took me to Central Station in Sydney and put me on the train for Brisbane. I can still clearly picture the train pulling out and me watching Dad get smaller and smaller as the platform disappeared into the distance.

Dramatic as that uprooting was, I have never hated my father for letting me go like that. Maybe it's because I have such limited memories of him — it's hard to hate someone if you hardly know them. Then again, it was a safer time, a safer generation and a safer Australia. Even though I was scared, I recall the train journey as being an adventure. It was a steep learning curve in the art of self-reliance. Mum wouldn't have approved, but it happened.

Fallout

When I reflect on my mother I think of country families, and particularly women, struggling against the shortages of resources and facilities and, of course, poor health services. My mother would probably have enjoyed a longer life if she had lived in Sydney and had access to better health care. I'm sure that battling as she did and having to make do motivated her to become an active member of the Country Women's Association (CWA) and to take part in a variety of voluntary work; her efforts included helping to establish the school bus service that picked up kids from the bush and got them to school in Condobolin.

My mum was a brave, clever woman who, having had seven children and two or three miscarriages, died at the age of thirty-eight. Tragically for her children, she was a victim of circumstances common to her generation. I only wish she had lived long enough for me to know her. I keep a photograph of her — standing in front of the old Condobolin State School bus — on my study desk at home to remind me every day of where I come from and to keep my feet on the ground. It's not a terribly good photograph, but I don't have many of Mum and this is among the best I've got.

In any event, my brothers, sisters and I are close. Losing a mother in childhood has at least that positive effect. Since 1984, we have spent every fourth Easter together. Our reunions have been held in Condobolin, Sydney, The Entrance (NSW), Brisbane (once at my home and once at my brother Arthur's place), and in 2004 in northern NSW.

UNDER NANA'S ROOF

Nana

Going to live with Nana and her second husband, Harry, who wasn't my real grandfather, held no special fears as I recall — to me at the time it was all a novelty. Nana was a good-hearted person, even if she was also a tough disciplinarian and intolerant in a number of respects.

My maternal grandmother had been born in 1896 and was eighty-four when she died in 1980. As a child of the late nineteenth century, she was a product of late Victorian values and the kind of upbringing that went with them. When World War I started she was a young woman. Her two brothers went and fought in France. She lived through the Depression, she lived through World War II, and by the time I came to be around, in the late 1950s, she was a woman who'd seen a lot of life. It's understandable that her generation, given their experiences, had a propensity for fearfulness and conservatism — for them, personal security was at such a premium.

Nana and Harry were pensioners who had not long been in Atherton, having moved off a small farm. So I blew into their lives just as they were settling into retirement. As well as doing charity work, Nana was involved with her network of friends. I can remember as a young person not being able to understand why she had the views she had. She used to think Robert Menzies was simply terrific. Nana had other typical conservative attitudes of the time — for example, she was opposed to trade unions.

Where I was concerned, Nana was firm but kind. She gave of her very best and supported me when I needed it. And she was also someone — not that we ever really sat down and discussed these sorts of things at any length — who valued education. Soon after I arrived at her place, she settled me into the local school, Atherton State School. I remember my first day there. There were all these kids to play with and I thoroughly enjoyed it, thought it was wonderful to have a bunch of kids to kick a ball with. I loved school, but I wonder how things would have gone for me had Nana not been a person of strong character, not risen to the challenge of raising me, not tightened her belt in order to cover the extra costs.

Busy days

Nana was a strong-willed person, and through her example she educated me to accept women as the equal of men. I was expected to pull my weight at home. My duties around the yard included mowing the lawn, gardening, feeding the chooks (everybody had chooks in those days) and bringing in the avocados (everybody had those, too); you weren't anybody if you didn't have your own garden and avocados! I also spent many an hour painting the house.

Nana was a powerful woman. An example:

A neighbour next door used to grow prickly cucumbers, which I hated, and I'd regularly be sent to collect a boxful of these dreadful things. As Nana passionately believed that you never left the table until you had eaten everything on your plate, I had to eat them. On the way home on my errand, a bit like in the Hansel and Gretel story, I would drop a long trail of these cucumbers until only half a box was left.

Nana wised up to what I was doing and I was horrified to return from school one day to find the half-full box now overflowing. Nothing was said. I knew the game was up. To this day I'm still lukewarm about cucumbers.

I struggle with my weight every day, so I'm not sure leaving a clean plate is good healthy eating. But Nana came from a generation that had to fight two World Wars and a Depression to survive. 'Waste not, want not' was her frequently repeated mantra.

She strongly believed in family, hard work and 'getting a good job'. Don't put off until tomorrow what you can do today, she regularly urged me. She believed a good work ethic is essential for a happy life. I came to realise that she was right.

The hardest workers were more likely to succeed at school, not always the brightest.

She instilled in me a passion for hard work and a determination to never give up when the going got tough: fighters are winners she believed, quitters are losers. But she also had a big heart. Her work for charity dominated her retirement years. She was personally very generous to her friends and family. She had a real country sense of community.

She was also a tough guardian. I was banned from school dances, prevented from regularly going to the movies and encouraged to attend church. We were Anglicans but sometimes I attended the Atherton Gospel Church. The church was fundamental, but caring and devoted. At the Gospel Sunday School we were taught to memorise passages from the Bible. (I learnt a memory technique there that I still use today.) They were good country people.

Later I became an altar boy at St Mary's Anglican Church. My job was to ring the gong at an appropriate point in the Communion service. Regrettably, I couldn't eat breakfast before Communion, so on two occasions I almost fainted during the service and had to be helped to a chair. A large drink of milk before the service soon solved the problem.

But Nana was also broadminded in many ways. A great mate of mine, Glen Graham, lived across the road. We had been friends for years and still are today. When I was in high school, Nana bought a new Holden Torana after she had been left a modest sum of money. On several occasions late at night Glen and I pushed the car quietly out of the garage and went for a spin. I look back and realise how stupid we were. The last time we did it, I got the car to 100 miles per hour on a straight road out of town. In doing so, I scared the hell out of both of us. That night Nana heard us pushing the car — at 2.00 a.m. — back into the garage. Nana called the police and I had to confess my sins. She was generous enough to forgive me, but my ears were ringing for months. I learnt my lesson.

While my Nana was something of a taskmaster, it wasn't all misery, and we certainly had our good times. Radio was a big thing when we were kids. And TV came while we were in Atherton, though the reception wasn't exactly up to scratch. But even if it had been better, I wouldn't have spent any extra time watching it because TV was definitely an indulgence — especially when I had to study or there was some work I had to do. As well as being tough, Nana had me organised from an early age, teaching me to make use of every moment.

Our situation

Without wishing to be melodramatic, my personal circumstances meant early life was sometimes difficult. Basin haircuts and hand-me-down clothes were the norm for me. Formal clothes or holidays were out of the question.

In early 1963 my grandmother applied to the State Children Department for monetary assistance and that year began to receive a small but steady flow of support for me which continued until I finished my schooling. In 2003, courtesy of Freedom of Information legislation, I requested the files held on me by the then Department of Families. Reading through those documents was an eye-opener.

First Nana had to fill out a form titled 'Application of a Female Relative, Other Than the Child's Own Mother, to Have a State Child Boarded-out With Her'. When they received the form, the State Children Department contacted the Inspector of Police in Cairns and requested him to 'cause inquiries to be made into her character and circumstances'. The practice of assessing whether a potential welfare recipient is a 'deserving case for assistance' has been around for a long time and still goes on today. It was sobering to discover the Department thought of us as 'cases', people whose bona fides had to be scrutinised. At the time, my Nana was just my Nana and I would have had no real sense of any difficulties she may have been experiencing in keeping me. Certainly, she never made me conscious of it.

Having been checked over by the police — a senior constable wrote the report and the Atherton station sergeant approved it — the department rubber-stamped the application and my grandmother was entitled to receive the grand sum of around £1/10s per week, or $3, towards my keep. There was still the matter of picking up the actual money itself. In order to be paid, it seems that Nana had to front up at the police station and put her hand out to one of the officers. Such was the way things were done back then.

What struck me was the sheer amount of paperwork that Nana had to do, not only at the outset but at regular intervals over the years. She completed dozens of forms, doggedly and faithfully, over a ten-year period. Judging by her handwritten answers to various form questions, she was literate to a basic rather than advanced standard, so this couldn't have been easy for her.

Nana taught me self-reliance, self-confidence and independence. She encouraged my education and a self-belief that I could succeed. But I have one huge regret that I carry even today. In mid-1971, Nana and I fell out over my arrest for protesting against the Springbok tour. She never really forgave me. Nor did she ever come to terms with my time as Secretary of the Queensland Railway Station Officers Union (1978–81) and my involvement with the ALP and the ALP Reform Movement. She disliked both the union movement and the ALP.

In late 1979 I was visiting North Queensland as part of a Union campaign and dropped in to visit her at home in Atherton. I had another official with me. It was the lowest point of our relationship. We argued about unions, the ALP — and almost everything else. It was a political and generational argument. I stormed out, angry, hurt and disappointed at the personal barbs. She died in early 1980 and I was still so angry about so many things she had said that I didn't go to her funeral.

A couple of years later I came to deeply regret my shallow, pigheaded and juvenile behaviour. I should have just copped what she said and let it go. I should have gone to her funeral or, more importantly, I should have made up with her while she was alive. I owe her so much.

But that clash with Nana profoundly changed me and ultimately made me a better person. My regret about my poor behaviour led me to never carry grudges. Some see this as a weakness in politics — I don't. Far better to argue in a constructive and positive way, and to respect the views of others. This knowledge sadly came at a price.

Atherton

Atherton was a conservative, small country town, one based on primary industries. It was a good community, it felt strong; I liked life there. Atherton was a place I came to love. Having arrived there because my family had been broken up, I still count myself lucky to have ended up in such a positive environment.

Life was far from boring — there were plenty of things for a kid to do. From an early age I was keen to involve myself in as many activities as I could. I played cricket, hockey and football; took part in athletics. Add to that list school theatrical productions, dramatic plays as well as Gilbert and Sullivan. And even though I couldn't sing, I did at one time land the role of Will Parker in *Oklahoma!* But it didn't matter that I couldn't sing — and that is an important point. Atherton meant opportunity, a chance to have a go.

Three powerful words: have a go. If it was possible back then in little Atherton, then it has to be possible throughout our society today. We should make it possible. You encourage kids to have a go — I believe this about our society generally, too — and out of that they acquire experiences. Some they learn from, some they don't.

An experience of possibilities was what Atherton gave me — the knowledge that you could go out and play sport or do well in class or whatever else you were involved in. Sure it could be competitive, people enjoyed that element, but it was also a warm society in the sense that you weren't ridiculed for trying.

When I was growing up there, Atherton had a quite diverse population. There were farmers who grew maize, and all sorts of other crops, including peanuts and potatoes. Plenty of farmers' kids went to my school. Retired people and small shopkeepers were among the other distinct groups in our community.

Many of the descendants of the Chinese who'd been to Palmer River and elsewhere searching for gold settled in the Atherton district and became retailers. The Fong Ons and Jue Sues spring to mind. So you had old Chinese families where the kids looked Chinese but spoke no Mandarin or Cantonese, just English. One of the highlights of 2002 for me was going up to Atherton and helping to open a newly restored Chinese temple — we'd have called it a joss house when I was a kid. It's on our new Heritage Trail Network, (part of a tourism development) which highlights and honours Queensland's heritage.

There were other significant populations in Atherton. Italians (because they'd been farmers there) Albanians and Yugoslavs were part of our community and went to my school. One of my best mates was a young fellow named Simon Elmas, better known as Sam. His mother was Lithuanian and his father was Albanian. Sam is a lovely guy with whom I've remained friends. The Kochis were a well-known Albanian family who are today significant in real estate on the Atherton Tableland. And, of course, Indigenous people were strong members of our community. At our school you were judged on who you were as a person.

More recently, I found it puzzling when Atherton became a stronghold for One Nation, a bizarre state of affairs if you look at the multicultural reality there. But I'm sure that, more than anything else, much of the vote for One Nation was an expression of voters' feelings of alienation from politics and political parties and political leaders. Atherton is more than 1800 kilometres from Brisbane. Distance and lack of access to government was a key factor in One Nation's support.

My early years in Atherton taught me about the strengths of living in a community made up of different kinds of people. Yet it was also my perception that things could have been better still. Newcomers may not have felt entirely welcomed in Atherton. It took time to assimilate into that community.

The people of Atherton were self-reliant types, and not just because farming communities are often that way inclined. Well into the '50s and '60s, people were still smarting over the idea that a 'Brisbane Line' had been discussed during World War II. Say the Japanese had invaded Australia, some top military hats had toyed with the idea of cutting our losses, writing off the population up north and defending Queensland at Brisbane. On that basis alone you can understand why north Queenslanders are sometimes described as parochial! But these figures from my childhood were strong people, the salt of the earth, and saw themselves as part of Australia's pioneering spirit.

Stand-outs

Despite the fact that Atherton was so far away from anything like metropolitan culture — it wasn't exactly the Paris of the North! — I had my share of influences. Certain experiences still really stand out for me.

When I was about thirteen, *Doctor Zhivago*, the movie, came to Atherton. At that age I hadn't read the novel that it was based on and I wasn't allowed out at night, but I did manage to sneak away to see *Doctor Zhivago* at the local flicks. What I saw knocked me out: humanity struggling against unjust systems — initially with the tsars, then communism, but also against the tyranny of the environment. Whenever I think of that movie, with all the cold and snow, I just about shiver! Here were human beings trying to live as people notwithstanding the harshness of the elements and the oppression that the political system exerted over them. I found the drama very affecting. Because it was such a long movie and I had to get home, sadly I didn't see it all. All these years later, I picture myself sitting there riveted, watching the scene where Zhivago walks down the line of telegraph posts in the cold. Another enduring image is of Zhivago chasing after the train in Moscow, trying to catch the woman he loved, and having a heart attack.

That film rammed home a keen sense of the drama that individuals sometimes have to endure when the system is destroying people. It may have been a romantic epic and, in the end, only a movie but it allowed me to see things through others' eyes. It helped develop my understanding of the individual, the family, the community and society.

Schooling

What I took away from *Doctor Zhivago* was a kind of learning unlike anything we were receiving through formal education back then. Learning things by rote and being able to recite the names of places or historical events or the great men of history — these things were the order of the day.

Nevertheless, for me school was always an exciting place, both Atherton State School and Atherton State High School, where I was to become school captain and dux in my final year. These were two good school communities, and also places where you had fun. Nana's place in Robert Street was directly across the road from the school. She tried to encourage me to come home for lunch but I strongly resisted. I wanted to play cricket with my mates — school was just too enjoyable. She eventually gave up trying.

Possibly the only downside was that the cane was still in use then in Queensland schools and I copped it a few times. I became bored easily, and to entertain myself and others on one occasion I made supersonic paper jets and tested their distance and reliability. Unfortunately, class was in session at the time. I was also once caned for playing the wrong drum beat as students marched into their classrooms. Thankfully as my interest in maths, science, history and English increased, my behaviour improved. I loved history and still do. I was the quietest pupil during history lessons.

I learnt how to high jump in primary school. Hour after hour, even on weekends, I practised the 'western roll' jump. It took me years to realise that I was just too short to be a great high jumper.

Receiving help from the state as we did, at the start of every school term I had to go round to the principal to collect my schoolbooks, which I didn't particularly like. No one else in the school seemed to be in the same position. As I grew older, it bothered me less. But while I could get on with my life, I also realised that my grandmother was doing it hard to raise me.

Occasionally, teachers appear who are able to make a difference in a young person's life. I was lucky in Atherton in that I had a number of committed teachers who knew — and understood — my personal circumstances and went out of their way to encourage me. Morrie Harnell, the principal of the high school, was the most prominent among them.

Mr Harnell, as we knew him back then, was someone who gave me positive support, and that was something I responded to well. When he died a couple of years ago, I didn't hesitate to cancel my appointments in order to attend his funeral.

While my own school days were very satisfying, I am acutely aware that that wasn't the case for everyone. For some of my peers, things didn't go so well after we left school. I think of a young guy called Milan Malokavich who I played cricket with and who was terrific at the shot put, a big-boned Yugoslav boy. After we did senior year, Milan was killed in a car accident, driving along a country road. I did not find out about his death for some years. I was saddened by the loss of a friend but also the loss of such a young life, snuffed out in a second. I knew then that life is not fair.

Wider horizons

In my senior year in 1970, I participated in the Lions Youth of the Year contest and made it through to the Australian finals, which were held in Canberra. To add to my excitement, I came fourth in the finals. My prize was a ten-day trip to Tasmania, which I took weeks later. I loved the place but more importantly the experience.

1970 was a huge year for me. Going to the nation's capital for the first time had been a fantastic experience. It was there that I first realised politics was a means through which you could change things. But I was doing my Senior Certificate, so it was time to set my sights on the next step. Unless they had a scholarship, students in the higher education system had to pay fees. After Whitlam won government at the end of 1972, such barriers would be removed. Students would be means-tested, and then people from my sort of background, economically speaking, would have the chance to get into university.

My mentor, Morrie Harnell, was encouraging me to be a teacher, which interested me, especially as my fees would be paid. But then I did very well in my final exams and there were new possibilities. I had always loved history, and law would be a good career I thought. The choice of law wasn't based on any personal experience — we had never had any lawyers in our family; indeed, I was the only one in my family who had ever had the chance to go to university. Luckily, I won a Commonwealth scholarship, which made it all possible.

At the start of the next year — 1971 — off I went to Brisbane, over eleven hundred miles (approximately 1800 km) from Atherton, to go to law school. I had an aunt who lived in Nundah in Brisbane. Other than her, I didn't really know anyone in Brisbane. So I decided to live at St John's College at the University of Queensland. I enrolled in Arts/Law and got on with the next phase in my life.

Arts/Law and St John's were my decisions, but made with Nana's support. I realise now she knew this was the right thing for my future. I know she was very proud of my achievements.

But looking back, my farewell from home was flat emotionally. I was leaving to conquer the world and Nana's job was done. She had given me a real chance at life, even if I was still too immature to know it. I wanted to get going, to take on the world and Nana knew she was going back to her real retirement. She wished me well, told me to work hard and stay out of trouble. I followed the first instruction.

Nana wasn't so lucky. In mid-1971 her second husband, Harry Esbensen, died. They only had six months of peace together.

MAKING MY WAY IN THE WORLD

University

In 1971, when I first set foot on the campus of the University of Queensland, I entered a whole new world. For a boy from 'the sticks', the general university environment itself was quite an awakening. People were wandering around in funny clothes, some of them smoking peculiar cigarettes. While dope-smoking was prevalent to an extent — and I certainly ran into people who indulged — it wasn't my scene. The dangers of drugs had been made clear to me; you just didn't do that.

Residential colleges were a little less 'out there' than the university at large, so from the relative shelter of St John's College, I eased into my new life.

Protest and change

1971 was a momentous year. It was the time of the anti-Vietnam War moratoriums. It was also the year when the Springboks toured Australia. When they came to Queensland, like many others I went along and protested. Why? I was eighteen and idealistic. It appalled me that people could be judged on the colour of their skin. Passionate about morality and justice, I couldn't accept that a person was bad, or was substandard, or in some ways in a different class because they were black, or that you could even promote the idea. While growing up, I'd developed a strong sense of fair play — the Australian spirit of a fair go. I was also a Christian. Christianity meant everyone was born equal in God's eyes. Colour had nothing to do with it.

The events of the Springbok tour and my involvement in protests against them proved to be a watershed for me. The Bjelke-Petersen government had strongly backed the team's visit and, by inference, supported the white-controlled South African apartheid government. It even announced a three-week state of emergency. The team was in Brisbane in July 1971 and a demonstration was organised to voice protest. I had been at university for just a few months and I had no other idea in my head than to contribute to making a point in a peaceful way. It would not have occurred to me to do anything other than behave peacefully. Having grown up in a country town that respected the law, I had faith in the police. I'd never had a run-in with them; I knew individual officers, didn't dislike them; and I had no axe to grind in their regard.

But when the police charged the protest march outside the Tower Mill Motel, where the team had been staying it was an awakening. Before my eyes people were bashed with batons, something I found very hard to understand. Then, when some of us went down the road to the old Trades Hall for sanctuary, the police came after us. They grabbed me and I was charged with disorderly conduct and resisting arrest! It was gobsmacking the way the charges were laid — I found myself being 'verballed' by the police who, in the washup, asserted fantasy as fact. Eventually, having sustained an injury to my back, I was taken off to hospital.

The details of the police charge gave me a jolt. No! This did not happen! Being a young law student, I knew the charges were minor. In the end, they were not proceeded with; the police just let it all go. Nevertheless, the painful reality I had been forced to confront was that the police had lied. This outraged my sense of justice. The police were supposed to keep the peace and tell the truth.

What lingered on, what kept niggling at me was the knowledge that the system was crook. We had to change it. I had been politicised by those events; they formed part of my maturing, too. At the same time, I'm not trying to glorify those days or suggest I was some heroic protest leader who resisted arrest.

Two details of that day are etched in my memory. In my mind's eye I replay the scene of a woman being bashed by a policeman with a baton and going head over heels down the hill — to someone brought up in a country town, and a touch chauvinistic, treating women like that goes against the grain. And my blood still boils when I remember that lies were put forward as fact in that statement.

At home, Nana was shocked and disappointed in me. Her country conservatism meant she never really forgave me. I had, in her eyes, become one of those university radicals. Tragically, our relationship never really recovered.

I also joined Young Labor that year, but whatever it was I'd expected to find there, I was disappointed. I didn't linger but found other things to do with my time and energy. The ALP would keep for later.

Campus life

As an undergraduate I studied as much as you had to and was self-disciplined to the extent that I always went to my lectures and tutorials — I wanted to get through and made sure I delivered my work. But I also had a good time, and campus life was enjoyable. Running as much for fun as anything, I was elected Secretary of the St John's Students' Club in 1973 and was then elected president in 1974, my last year there. I was involved in the college and was hugely into sport — inter-college competition in hockey for a while, rugby union, and rugby league for the university. I also took part in debating.

There was a good cultural life at college. The now former

Anglican Primate of Australia, Dr Peter Carnley, was college warden for two of my four years at St John's. I liked him and admired his warmth, tolerance and humility, even though we didn't always agree. I immersed myself in the broader university life through the law. Government and history were my majors — they are still my passions — and I finished up with a BA, LLB. (I received an MA more recently in 1997 for a thesis I did on the Fitzgerald Inquiry. I was undertaking a doctorate but when I became health minister I knew I would never finish, so converted it to an MA.)

During my student years, I remained true to my roots. If ever there was a dollar or two spare, I was not inclined to go out and spend it on booze or a good time in general. If you've grown up not having money, you think twice about being extravagant. In many ways I'm still what might be termed 'traditionally Presbyterian'. Perhaps it's my Scots ancestry coming into play. In any event, I was definitely a young person who placed some value on restraint.

While I was at university I met up with a friend from Atherton days, Heather Scott-Halliday. Together in 1973 and 1974, Heather and I did the rounds of the college 'At Homes'. Colleges provided a great social life. But, as two country kids at heart, there was no marijuana and no wild parties — just moderate ones.

College was an easy place to make friends. Country kids dominated the residential colleges and this led to special bonds. We were all in this together.

A number of us bonded together in our fresher year to avoid being 'laked'. This was the sad practice — now banned — of stripping the clothes of some 'obnoxious' fresher and throwing them naked into the university lake in front of one of the women's colleges. They would then have to run naked back to college. Not very mature behaviour!

My debating team friends were especially close and they were keen debaters. We won the inter-college debating competition in 1974, my presidential year.

Love and marriage

Heather was in Grade 8 and I was in Grade 9 when we met at school in Atherton. I was strongly attracted to her. She was intelligent — she won a Commonwealth scholarship in Grade 10, something outrageously difficult to do — she was kind, considerate, warm, compassionate, and not only was she all those things but we felt an affinity for one another.

Heather's dad was an Anglican minister, and the family had lived in Proserpine and Mount Isa before coming to Atherton. Her father wasn't that well. The family was only in Atherton a couple of years, and his health deteriorated afterwards. When Heather and her family moved to Charleville, she and I kept in touch.

Her father died in January 1973. Just one month earlier, he'd agreed to Heather's and my engagement when I asked his permission while I was on a visit to Charleville.

Heather and I were married on 4 January 1975. Ours was a small, modest wedding. We invited our university friends to Redcliffe, where we had a very pleasant celebration. There was no sense of rushing into anything. Nor did we go into marriage with any sort of big plan. In addition to experiencing those strong feelings of love and emotion that are so important, we got on really well. We liked and admired one another and we were always complementary, easy with each other. As for children, we talked about whether we'd have them or not, and decided yes, but that would be for later.

Finding our feet

When we got married, I was an articled law clerk and Heather was a trainee nurse. With scarcely two pennies to rub together, we had to build up our funds. For the first couple of years of our married life we lived in a two-room, one-bedroom flat on Fernberg Road, Rosalie, just down the hill from the Governor's official residence. Ours was the kind of place where, if you'd swung the proverbial cat round, you would most certainly have knocked off its head.

The couple who owned the property, Tom and Jean Daley, were lovely people. They didn't know us from Adam, but they must have felt sorry for us, thinking here's this young couple starting off who don't know anything. They took us under their wing, and we got on well with them. Tom and Jean had moved up from Melbourne and invested in flats. Ironically, it was our landlords who went out of their way to encourage us to buy a home. This could hardly have been in their financial interests because we were probably the ideal pair of tenants. We always paid our rent, we were hardly noisy, we didn't have wild parties.

What Jean and Tom impressed upon us was the value of investments and of saving a percentage of your income. Consequently we took some deep breaths and went house-hunting. Jean and Tom gave us good feedback about the home we picked out, and were there with advice and support when it was needed. Being a couple of country kids, Heather and I didn't know anything about buying a house in Brisbane, but it turned out to be one of the smartest things we ever did. We sorted out a mortgage and bought a worker's cottage on a huge block of land in Milton. We paid $23,000 — an absolute fortune, or so it felt to us at the time. But from the standpoint of financial security, we never looked back.

We lived there for fifteen years. During this time we had the house extended and our three children, Larissa and twins Matthew and Denis, were born. The three of them arrived within a period of fourteen months. The demands of my political career had already ramped up considerably, leaving Heather with a massive load, managing the children and keeping everything rolling along.

Milton contains so many memories: Denis falling off the back verandah and being rushed to hospital on the eve of my maiden speech in Parliament; the children walking for the first time, losing their first teeth; my election to Parliament on 2 December 1989. Our dreams and lifelong plans were formed at Milton; our first home was special.

Gough

Looking back, the ingredients that gave me the drive to get into politics are easy to spot. For starters, there were my early circumstances and the influence of my grandmother. Then came exposure to new ideas at university, the shock of seeing how power could be misused, as in the Springboks episode — these were the sorts of experiences that were accumulating as I grew up, sparking the desire to work at developing policies that remedied injustices and improved life for the greater number of people.

There was another key influence — Gough Whitlam. Winning government after twenty-three years of conservative rule, Whitlam was the first political leader who mattered to me. Whitlam talked about things that I could relate to; he spoke of education, a fair go for all, advancing the interests of women, helping to improve people's lives in the communities in which they live, and a great many other things. He talked about issues that meant something, particularly education. The universal health cover represented by Medibank was also significant to me because I observed the struggles of my grandmother when she wasn't terribly well and getting into her seventies. At the time we did have a free hospital system in

Queensland, but universal health care was unknown, so finding the money for doctors' fees was often difficult for poorer people.

I thought Whitlam was inspired in many ways. As an eighteen- or nineteen-year-old, like any teenager, I wasn't familiar with political processes and knew little of Gough Whitlam's battles within and on behalf of the Labor Party. But later, when I did learn of his history in the ALP and the efforts he made to reconstruct the Party when it was going through one of its doldrum periods, I was all the more impressed.

An interest in politics

At university I began a more formal political education of sorts, inasmuch as I studied the governments of Australia, the United States and the Soviet Union. I also rapidly came to the conclusion that student politics were, to say the least, a juvenile business. It seemed to be about little more than the struggle for positions. I didn't really like that or find it engaging, just as I'd found nothing about Young Labor in 1971 that compelled me to become involved.

But the lead-up to the 1972 federal election and the impact that federal Labor was making on the electorate generally gave me hope, as it did a lot of other people. When voting day came around, I was with Heather in Charleville, where her sister was getting married. I remember hearing the result on the radio after the wedding.

After a couple of years on the sidelines — although always watching what was going on with keen interest — I applied to join the Party proper at the end of 1974. From then on I was a regular member of the Rosalie branch in the electorate of Ithaca, in the inner-western suburbs of Brisbane, a one-time staunchly Liberal seat but one that no longer exists. My membership dates from 1 January 1975. What prompted me to sign up? I wanted to become involved in trying to improve things. Young though I was, I had a conviction that health and education needed fixing.

Little did I realise at the time just how involved I was to become. My political career was about to begin.

Part II

UP THROUGH THE RANKS

The Canberra trip of 1970 had been a factor in my becoming interested in politics. Back then I believed in destiny. I planned and plotted and slaved away. Early on I was driven by an obsession to make my part of the world a better place and a self-belief that I was the best person to do it. Today, thankfully, I am wiser and mellower: I believe in hard work and good luck.

From the time I joined the Australian Labor Party at the very end of 1974, I quickly became absorbed by the political process, its intricacies, its challenges, its capacity to shape people's destinies. But the Party in Queensland wasn't doing well. It was run by simply too small a group — it wasn't inclusive enough, there weren't enough women, there weren't enough people of ethnic background involved, and there wasn't a good administration. The ALP in Queensland was closed in on itself, and far too narrowly based. It needed opening up. We had to shake it up. And we did. In December 1977 I helped initiate the Reform Movement in the Labor Party.

My life in politics gathered momentum through the latter half of the 1980s. By then I had become secretary of the ALP in Queensland and, after more than thirty years in Opposition, we were starting to look like a real possibility for government.

In retrospect, the various experiences and knock-backs before that time, such as being gagged while still secretary and failing to win a preselection, were a kind of toughening up ahead of the more important challenge: achieving government, then being in government.

BECOMING ABSORBED
IN POLITICS

At the grassroots level

Crystal clear in my memory are those early Rosalie branch meetings. I was a regular attendee. Even if sometimes the meetings were as boring as hell and mainly about procedural matters or very small-scale local issues, for me they were an education. It has become fashionable in some circles today to criticise aspects of branch life. But it's there that ordinary people have an opportunity to express their views, and that was how I experienced it.

At times branch involvement was riveting for all present — we had strong local party members, and they used to debate the questions of the day — what was happening not only with

Premier Joh but nationally. The local branch provided plenty
of opportunity for people to talk about policy issues, too.
Personally, I was keen on general business, and agenda items
were always useful for stimulating debate.

I was driven. I wanted the ALP to win an election and
implement better policies. Perhaps it was just youthful
enthusiasm, but I always believed we could and would do it.
I clearly remember this self-belief. We had been losers since
1957. I believed Queensland deserved something more than
the Bjelke-Petersen government and the then incompetent
ALP. I wanted change for the better, but I knew we needed
change within the ALP first; I realised this soon after joining.
We were out of touch and out of government as a result.

The home front

Heather knew I was obsessed with politics and that I wanted to
change our little part of the world. Early on, we weren't sure
how to do it. We talked and talked about policy, how bad the
Bjelke-Petersen government was in key areas like education
and social spending. Heather joined the ALP not long after I
did and was a full partner in my obsession. But she was gentler
and shy; I'm sure her warm personality made it harder for my
detractors to attack me. Together we became ALP slaves to
prove our genuineness and worth.

After having children it was harder. I had to do the political
work more and more on my own, but still with Heather's

support. Without her taking on the role of chief parent, our plans would have collapsed. By 1986, we had three children under two (with the twins). Heather's enormous intellectual, mental and physical capacity held our family and political lives together. She had a little daughter, twin sons (fourteen months younger), a driven husband and a career, and she handled the whole lot brilliantly. I couldn't have done it alone.

Had Heather's father not been so sick in her final year of school, she might have studied medicine or architecture. She was close to her father; his having unstoppable cancer had been traumatic for her. In the end, Heather chose her mother's career of nursing. She earned a hospital certificate in nursing, followed by a diploma of applied science, a bachelor's degree in nursing and a Masters in Education. To top it off, she achieved her Doctorate of Education, and is now an Associate Professor of Nursing at the University of Queensland. Heather has done incredibly well and she's done it all the hard way.

We've both had to pull ourselves up by the bootstraps. Whatever we set out to achieve, the foundation for our future lives has basically lain in our education and training, and subsequently the ability to save a little money over the years.

Heather shares many of my interests. She likes people, she likes government, she likes helping people. Although she had no political ambitions of her own, then or now, she was twice elected as a branch representative from the federal seat of

Brisbane to the ALP's State Council. Heather has a good head for policy and, while she is more reserved than me, loves a debate. She is a natural leader in any policy discussion.

While Heather has been utterly supportive of my goals in and through the Labor Party, like a lot of politicians' spouses nowadays she loathes some aspects of politics with a passion. And for good reason — I'm hardly ever home, for starters. The quagmire of party politics is a cesspit of disenchantment for any ideologically positive person; it can be the deathbed of idealism.

Heather has raised our three kids largely on her own, and with all the difficulties that entails. Where both partners have jobs or careers, that constant juggling of individual and family needs inevitably involves enormous pressures; they seem to be endemic to modern life. I'm not sure what the answer is.

One thing I do know is that although she has been fantastically encouraging of me, Heather will breathe a sigh of relief when I retire. We've been together thirty years, been through the ups and downs that any relationship goes through, but we're still nuts about each other and look forward to spending more time together.

The Dismissal, a chance to observe and learn

As a member of the Party and an admirer of Whitlam, I was stunned when he was dismissed. To me, Whitlam stood for a new Australia. He was active in promoting tolerance; he used to speak to all kinds of communities, including the big Greek community we have in Queensland. Here was a man who loved history and talked about it in a way that suggested you could definitely learn from the past. He was very learned, and that was something I always admired about him and found personally inspiring. Later, I enjoyed getting to know Gough personally and I still see him from time to time.

In terms of policies, Whitlam hadn't just talked about them — he delivered on education; he delivered on health; the same goes for many other areas. I believe he changed Australia as much as any single person can. He was prime minister for less than three years, but it was long enough to make a profound difference. So I realised that you don't always need great periods of time to effect positive change (Mike Ahern, an honest and decent man, was the National Party premier here for less than two years and changed certain things for the better both during and after the Fitzgerald Inquiry). Federally, Gough Whitlam lit a torch which no one has ever been able to put out.

There was much to be learnt from Whitlam and the Dismissal. I was idealistic and certainly Gough was my hero, then and now. But we all had to grasp the very important lesson — and this was Bob Hawke's great addition to the picture — that you have to be able to manage the economy; you've got to be able get the figures right. John Faulkner's television interview with Whitlam[1] gave a fascinating alternative view of the Whitlam economic performance — even if the view was Whitlam's own! He pointed out that interest rates were lower at the time, he went through the various economic achievements of his government and justified its financial credibility. I leave to others to decide whether he was on the mark or not.

The reality is that the economic dynamics of a country can't be changed in a short period. There are waves and cycles which we know are beyond the control of any individual mortal. But, economics apart, Whitlam was vilified for some pretty base reasons, one being that he had the hide to be the first Labor prime minister since 1949, the first bloke from that side in twenty-three years — and for that the conservatives were prepared to destroy him. Nevertheless, Gough paved the way for the future.

After Gough, the drive to rebuild

For Labor, the loss of government in 1975 had many repercussions, not only federally but at state level. As a member of the Rosalie branch I had met the federal member for Brisbane, Manfred Cross, and was keenly disappointed when he lost that seat in the general backlash in 1975. Manfred was a true Laborite, someone who had a strong sense of the importance of good structures to the functioning — and fortunes — of the party over time. From him I got the message about the fundamental need for effective party administration.

After the dip in morale that Labor people experienced following 13 December 1975, there was soon plenty of impetus for those who wanted to see the Party make a recovery. I found myself becoming more serious about formal politics.

The state election was held in 1977. I became campaign director for the local state candidate to prove my commitment and learn how to campaign. By the end of 1977, I had become involved in administrative restructure and policy development in the Labor Party in Queensland. Tom Burns was state leader, and he pulled together something of a think tank to develop ideas and policy. Burns was good at bringing people together to try to work out a way forward and so started to open things up. From that point, the reform movement — and my life as a political player — began to develop in earnest.

AGITATING FOR CHANGE,
1977-81

The need for reform

As a campaign director in 1977, I was into politics boots and all. I was committed to the ALP in all senses — by temperament, values and logic — and I hated to see the Party lose its rightful place in the government of this country. The fact that we didn't do well at a federal and state level frustrated me greatly. However, I had long since asked myself what it was about the Queensland ALP that wasn't working as well as it might have been.

As I've written elsewhere,[1] the Labor Party in Queensland in the 1970s was struggling with that most basic of questions: who do we represent? Older voices, some of them less relevant than they had once been, were still being listened to first and foremost, while new voices — those of women, small business people, academics, white-collar unionists and others — were growing in number and importance as elements in the Party but were scarcely being heard. Consequently, these newer supporters had little input into our policies. How to let in the new aspirations and needs of these people — who, after all, looked to the ALP for leadership, not to the coalition parties — was a burning question for me. Fortunately, there were a number of like-minded people around at the time.

From very early on, my take on Oppositions has been that they cannot deliver visions for the future — only governments can do that. My view was that the glories of Opposition were limited and that in fact they didn't exist. Yet in the late 1970s I observed that we had an Opposition culture in the Party and that people found it hunky-dory just to be members of parliament. Worse still, some of our members were positively terrified of government, either because it meant doing some work or they were terrified of the challenges generally. Unfortunately, this situation has cropped up in Australian Labor Party history and politics from time to time.

Another of the obstacles to be overcome before Labor in Queensland would ever see government again was the tall poppy syndrome within its own ranks. For instance, there was a debate in the Party about whether you were genuine working class or not. To be 'working class' was far better than any alternative, such as being an 'academic' — the latter meant you were conceited, not the sort of person some in the Party wanted.

Hang on, I thought, this is ridiculous. Surely one thing our parents and our families were on about was better education for working kids to give us a better chance in life. Suddenly, working kids make it and get to university, and then just as suddenly they're treated as if they've broken ranks and aren't good enough. As well, some of the old diehards believed that if you weren't working for a trade union you couldn't be genuine working class, which was a phoney argument of the worst order.

It has been a theme in my life to try to avoid being judgmental. Education is not the final determinant of people's life chances or their worth. And just because someone has an education doesn't necessarily mean they're smart. On the other hand, just because you've missed out on an education doesn't mean you're stupid either. These things I learnt from within my own family. My brother Arthur, who always went out of his way to support me emotionally and materially, is a great example. He flew me out to join him in New Guinea a couple of times when he was working there, and he used to help me out a bit. Arthur finished school at Grade 8, yet he's brighter than I'll ever be. And he's a successful self-made businessman.

Those long-held beliefs informed my desire to push for change in the Queensland ALP. Never did I feel that the relative lack of higher training and higher education backgrounds among some Labor people at the time was any impediment to re-engineering the Party.

Mentors — Manfred Cross and Denis Murphy

In the late '70s, there were plenty of good people capable of turning the Party around. Manfred Cross was my mentor in the Party. He taught me the value of local grass-roots campaigning, of valuing party membership while also respecting people for who they are. Manfred was the federal member for Brisbane from 1961 to 1990, with a Whitlam-enforced break between 1975 and 1980. He was also the first Queensland ALP state secretary after federal ALP intervention into the Queensland branch in 1980. He was, therefore, my predecessor as ALP secretary. Manfred's wife, Barbara, was a strong influence on Heather's early Party activities. Later she became godmother to our daughter Larissa, who still affectionately calls her Grandma Barbara.

Another of those to whom I looked up and who helped rehabilitate the Party was Dr Denis Murphy. Born in Nambour into a working-class family — he was one of eight children, his father a labourer — Denis had gone on to gain a higher education at the University of Queensland, eventually completing a doctorate in history. As a lecturer at the University of Queensland, Denis Murphy would eventually be the only 'academic' to become president of the Labor Party in Queensland.

Denis played a key role in showing me how the past might be used to inform a more positive future for Queensland. He was the nearest thing to being the ALP's 'historian' in Queensland, and more than that he demonstrated an understanding and love for the Party and its role in society that was inspirational to all who came across him.

Drawing on his scholarly knowledge of the history of the ALP in the state, Denis had written, among other books, a biography of T.J. Ryan, an early Labor premier.[2] With Denis I was able to discuss Ryan's reforms in the sugar and other industries and what he had done in key areas that had resulted in improving people's lives.

In essence, during the late '70s and early '80s, Denis Murphy taught me the Labor Party heritage, something for which I'll always be grateful.

The start of the push

With Denis's involvement, it was decided to hold a meeting to discuss how we might reinvigorate the Party and find a new way forward to government. Pat Comben (later Minister for the Environment and Heritage then Minister for Education in the Goss government) and I organised a gathering of Party members in Indooroopilly for 11 December 1977. That meeting, which took place around a barbecue, was — ironically — the day after yet another federal electoral failure for our side.

Despite having invited as many people as we could, we were pleasantly surprised when eighty or so turned up. Unfortunately at that first meeting I was forced to do without Murphy's wisdom and contribution as he wasn't able to make it, although he was there for our next encounter. Those who attended that afternoon wanted change and were heartily tired of losing. They brought with them all shades of Labor opinion, and there was much sound talk on how Labor in Queensland might turn itself into a positive choice for the voters, not just perennial easybeats for the coalition parties.

A steering committee of thirteen, including Denis Murphy and me, was appointed with a brief to further the cause of reform. Our immediate task was to arrange a future and larger session.

Shaping the reform agenda

Reform is painful. The short version of the events that unfolded is that the then federal leader Bill Hayden came onside; there was a lot of argy-bargy, which eventually occasioned federal intervention; a new administration was set up; and the rest, as they say, is history. That summary, however, goes nowhere near to conveying the slog, the highs and lows.

So let's go back to 1978. The Reform Group steering committee issued a general invitation to all ALP members to attend a meeting at the Bardon RSL Hall on 5 March that year, to discuss the future of the Party. Several hundred turned up looking for hope, for a way forward.

The Party controllers sent along their spies after first threatening to expel anyone who attended. The size of the gathering killed any expulsion threats.

Denis Murphy's contribution was typically thorough and researched. He gave us chapter and verse on the Party's failures and inadequacies in its administration. The meetings of the Queensland Central Executive (QCE) were long and poorly run. Record keeping and budgetary reporting were unknown. There were no records of correspondence. Nobody even knew how much the Party was worth financially. In so thoroughly and professionally enumerating the QCE's failures and shortcomings, Denis gave me a strong platform from which to make my own contribution.

I picked up on the theme of inadequate representation. It seemed far more productive to plead the case for wider inclusion of members in policy matters and the running of the Party than to tackle the Party leadership head-on. 'We are not anti-union,' I stressed, 'we are simply asking for a more representative and efficient QCE and Inner Executive ... We are ordinary members of the Labor Party who are sick and tired of an unresponsive, dictatorial Inner Executive.'[3]

That widely reported meeting was the first stage of building pressure on the ALP National Executive and federal leader Bill Hayden to reform the incompetent Queensland branch.

Soon the term 'federal intervention' started to be bandied about within the Party. In July 1978, an investigation into the ALP's Queensland structure and administration was put in place. A team led by Party President, Neil Batt, and National Secretary, David Combe, eventually reported in September, recommending the replacement of the QCE by a state council, one based on a ratio of 60:40 trade union delegates to others and an expansion of the Inner Executive, taking its numbers from seven to fifteen.

Frankly, those changes had no effect on the vital question of enhanced representation, particularly as first-past-the-post voting was retained. Further, thanks to the re-affiliation of the Australian Workers' Union in 1978, the old group found itself 'reinvigorated' — on the numbers front, if nowhere else.

A special convention that we had proposed, which was to have been held by the end of 1978, never eventuated. Instead, the date of the planned QCE convention in Rockhampton was brought forward several months to February 1979. At that event our Reform Group found itself comprehensively rolled on almost all our initiatives.

Nevertheless, we had also become protagonists in the battle for the high ground — and we had won some support, both within the state ALP machine and federally.

As tension built to pressure-cooker proportions in the Party, the Old Guard refused to budge. Bill Hayden, also a member of the Inner Executive of the QCE, and incensed by the obstreperous attitude of one of his fellow executive members, offered at the Party conference in Rockhampton in 1979 to stand down 'as an example that someone else might follow'.[4] The anti-reformist member failed to take the bait.

Hot blood

The steering committee was taking a direct approach to reform because we were frustrated and keen to change the Party in Queensland. My own approach could be described as extremely determined, if not impetuous. There was open revolt within the Queensland Labor Party. But a lot of this energy was about winning — not for winning's sake but in order to implement policies in education and health, and to do all the things that were central, as I saw it, to the purpose of the Labor Party. And central, really, to who I was and am as a person.

In retrospect, we would all probably do things a little more calmly these days. Still, maybe if we had we wouldn't have achieved the results that we did. My common reaction to the intransigent and negative attitudes that were put up against proposals for positive change was to become hot under the collar.

For his part, Denis Murphy displayed a more patient and incremental approach to righting the obvious wrongs in our Party. He took the defeat far more philosophically than I did. When some of us in the Reform Group reassembled after the rebuff of our first attempt at restructure, Denis found it impossible to support us and we lost his involvement — not so much with the ends we all shared, but with the means we had chosen. Denis was prepared to be patient. We were not. We wanted change there and then.

Working in the law

In 1975 — the year Heather and I married, and when I also became a keen member of the ALP — I was an articled law clerk. In order to qualify to practise law, I had to do another year at university, followed by two more years of articled clerkship. Lining up articles was difficult — the system has since changed; it's even harder now — and I was lucky enough to do my articles with a good firm called McCullough Robertson. It was, and still is, a large firm in Queensland terms, and it had various departments. During that two-year stretch I did a fair bit of common law as well as some estate planning. Although I was modestly paid, I was 'rewarded by experience', as the saying goes. It was a very positive time.

McCullough Robertson was a traditional style of firm, and it acted for a number of conservative clients. Having someone like me around — someone who was actively involved in the Labor Party — was probably a little difficult for them and, although there was never ever discussion about it, I came to think I should look around for something else. In January 1978 I was admitted as a solicitor. After that, I did a brief stint with Australia's oldest national finance company, the Australian Guarantee Corporation — better known as the AGC — as their company solicitor in Brisbane. By this stage, I only had a little corporate work experience under my belt. Of course, in those days you could almost be guaranteed a job of some sort; if my memory serves me, unemployment was running at around two per cent, practically negligible. The question wasn't whether you found a job but rather where you found one. Today the picture is vastly different. You have to have a set of transferable skills in order to have a half decent chance of sustaining employment or developing a career.

From my sojourns at McCullough Robertson and at the AGC, I took away one lesson that stood out from everything else: I loathed family law. Disputes between couples, as tackled through the courts, served to highlight for me the thin line between love and hate. It was also most depressing to see children used as pawns in marriage break-ups.

Union secretary

Much as I wanted to see change come quickly to the Queensland ALP, I began to understand that that wasn't the way the world always worked. I would have to learn patience, the lesson that Denis had tried to teach us when things didn't go our way or to the timetable we had in our own heads. Life had to go on, even for me. After just a few months in early 1978 as company solicitor for the AGC, I was looking to work in the arena where I felt I could make some difference: the political world.

Fortunately, there arose an opportunity to get involved in another area of political activity, this time in defending and supporting the rights of workers in the Queensland railways. In April that year I applied for and won the position of secretary of the Queensland Railway Station Officers Union. In so doing, I qualified as a unionist and hence a 'non-academic' in the eyes of the Party's Old Guard. For the three-and-a-half years I represented the union, I attempted to prove to them that lawyers could be good unionists, too. I believed in trade unions but I also believed in the rights of the children of working-class families to reach their full potential, and that if they did they should be embraced by the Party, whether they were lawyers, teachers, doctors or trade union secretaries.

I was the one who had my eyes opened, however. For me, this new area of work provided a real lesson as to why we needed not only an Australian Labor Party but an Australian Labor Party in government. As I set about schooling myself on the situation and conditions in which the staff of railway stations had to work, my awareness grew about the effect that reactionary politics and general neglect could have on the welfare of working people.

Especially in the distant country stations, conditions were nothing less than Dickensian. To give an example: on one research trip through the southwest I discovered that at least one-third of the railway houses, the employees' living quarters, still had backyard toilets of the unsewered variety. Outhouses of this sort might have been acceptable back in the Middle Ages but they were entirely inappropriate to twentieth-century living and were an insult to the employees who had to put up with them. As well, many houses were in general disrepair and there was a widespread lack of hot running water.

Working conditions like these had a predictable effect on the morale of railway employees, meaning that many good people who were an asset to the organisation left when and where they could and took their experience with them. This deplorable situation was mainly the result of the underfunding and general under-resourcing of the railways by previous state governments. To me, that lack of support showed the Liberal–National Party government's contempt for ordinary working people so typical of the time.

Once I'd got the bit between my teeth, there was no stopping me. I made it my business to get the message across to government, and really anyone who would listen, as effectively as I could — much to the annoyance of the powers that were at the time. In the process of trying to improve the lot for my union constituency, I picked up some early useful lessons on how to highlight issues in the media to get a point across, lessons that have stood me in good stead.

As state secretary I visited almost every railway station in the state. In the process I came to understand Queensland, its regions, the bush, the size of the state and the tyranny of distance. In short I got to know Queensland well. It was a key part of my education and I loved it.

The friends I made in the Railway Station Officers Union last to this day. The president, Les Turner, was a working station master and a terrific bloke. Whenever the union council or executive made a decision, everyone was loyal to the decision and tried to make it succeed. It's a pity that that doesn't happen nearly as often in party politics.

Professional politician

My railways experience was interesting and invaluable but I realised after a time that I was still keen to get into formal politics. This ambition, however, was to be further thwarted — at least for a while. I had been less than cautious in criticism of a few members of the parliamentary Labor Party, and found that some were offended at being described as 'inept' or 'dead wood'.

In 1979 I was called before the QCE, the old Inner Executive of the ALP, and told to explain myself. I was suspended from the Party for three months and had to appeal to the National Executive for re-admittance.

I was perfectly happy to stand by my assessment of the quality of some of our own people — and I was not alone in that assessment. However, the three months I would have to spend in quarantine did mean that I was short of the qualifying period of three continuous years' membership required before you could stand for preselection as an ALP candidate or delegate to conference.

As this suspension had been handed to me by the recalcitrant state branch at the time, it did beg the obvious response — an appeal to the federal Party. An appeal on this basis was always an option for anyone who wanted to stand as a federal candidate. And that was the course I chose to take. To get my matter before the National Executive I needed to be a federal candidate, so I nominated for the safe Liberal federal seat of Ryan. Although it might be argued I was playing politics within my own party, I felt I would find support in the higher councils of the Party and this proved to be correct when, on 26 October 1979, the Federal Executive voted to turn my suspension into a reprimand. As a result I was obliged to stand for the House of Representatives seat of Ryan, at that time a traditional Liberal stronghold in Queensland.

My one-time run at a federal seat taught me a great deal about the realities of being a candidate. I learned much about on-the-ground grassroots candidacy, of listening to and dealing with the real people who also happen to have power over your personal political fate. In the end, Ryan was not to be mine — but then again no one, not even me, truly expected that it would. Although I ended with 34 per cent of the vote, the real achievement was in securing a swing in all sub-divisions bar St Lucia, and that was satisfying enough in itself. However, my own little political drama was soon to pale against what was about to happen on the bigger ALP stage.

Achieving reform

Things were finally coming to a head in the increasingly tortured relations between federal Labor and the Queensland branch. The 1978 foray into reform had gained a little ground, but leader Bill Hayden was now prepared to push for more serious intervention. On 1 March 1980 a list of seventeen National Executive charges against the Queensland branch led to the Federal Executive voting 11–7 for intervention. As that process unfolded, the local committees were dismantled and an Interim Administrative Committee, which included Manfred Cross, me and Denis Murphy, was appointed. At that point, things got truly interesting.

The previous administration refused to accept the umpire's decision and resolved that it wasn't going anywhere. The diehards would not be moved from the Party's old headquarters at Breakfast Creek, obliging us to begin our own work from a new site in Charlotte Street. The 'Breakfast Creek mob' then thought there was value in challenging us in the Supreme Court, a move that meant progress on reform was further held up.

The final nail in the coffin of the Old Guard and its attitudes had to wait until our 1981 State Conference. There, the reformists, led by Denis Murphy, were finally able to prevail fully and convincingly, winning nine of the fifteen administrative committee positions and gaining proper control over the affairs of the Party. There were a number of other positives that flowed with this majority, including the election of six women to the administrative committee, double the guaranteed three that the ALP Federal Executive had approved early in June. But it was only when Mr Justice Lucas handed down his decision, on 2 July 1981, granting legitimacy to the new administration, that we finally felt victory was ours.

HARD YARDS,
1981–86

State secretary

In September of 1981, at the urging of Manfred Cross and Denis Murphy, I succeeded Manfred in the role of state secretary of the ALP in Queensland, as he was returning to federal parliament. Personally I hadn't considered the job but Manfred and Denis, keen for the momentum of reform to continue, were full of encouragement. It was a time for celebration: we'd made it; we'd achieved reform; and we were running the Party at last.

Then to work. The Reform Group, dubbed the New Guard, split into two factions. One was the Socialist Left. I went with the Centre Left, a term coined by Party member Bernie

McKenna. We saw ourselves as a moderating group in the old argument between Left and Right Labor.

Now began the long haul towards winning government.

It won't happen overnight, but . . .

The Queensland ALP had a fair number of tasks to be going on with. We wanted to reform administration, to find strong candidates, to develop good and appealing policies, to make the Party responsive to women, to open it up to new and different groups and to broaden the base. That kind of a 'to do' list was always going to take time. And that's without mentioning the over-arching reality of life in Queensland.

Joh Bjelke-Petersen and the National Party held the reins of power in the state. The most effective political machine in Australia, they were constantly at our backs with daggers drawn. Instead of wasting emotion on despising them, we studied their success and homed in on what was useful.

Our first chance to apply some of these ideas was during the 1983 state election. It marked the start of a new style of campaign for Queensland Labor. Our mood was buoyant. Federally, things were going well for the Party. In 1983, Bob Hawke had become Prime Minister of Australia, so Labor was back in power for the first time since the fall of the Whitlam government.

At a state level, we were able to put forward some fresh and appealing new candidates, including Wayne Goss. David

Hamill, Denis Murphy and I worked with the caucus drafting policy documents and organising for them to be released with caucus approval. This didn't always go as well as we would've liked, but we were getting better all the time.

We went into the election with a huge campaign launch at the Greek Community Centre in South Brisbane. Public polling ahead of the election day suggested we were picking up momentum, but then in the final stages the Nationals sucker-punched us with statistics involving some government charges they had supposedly found in Labor-run states. Although we had no local taxation policies that could be challenged, the Nationals' well-timed media blitz left us reeling as the media focused on that perennial political bogeyman, the high-taxing Labor mob. In the end, we picked up seven seats, which meant we had thirty-two seats in the eighty-two-seat Assembly. Disappointingly, Mt Isa aside, none of our new seats had come from where we really needed them — the National Party heartland. Nevertheless, it was gratifying to know that both Denis Murphy (Stafford) and Wayne Goss (Salisbury) were about to enter parliament for the first time, as were David Hamill, Keith De Lacey, Patrick Comben and Anne Warner.

It was the Liberals who were the great losers of that election, giving up seats to both our side and the Nationals. And because the Liberal leader, Terry White, had torn up the Coalition agreement, Joh did not achieve the majority he needed to govern alone until three days after the election, when two Liberals agreed to join with him.

An untimely death

Denis Murphy was more than just an excellent academic and Labor historian. He understood Queensland. He could see the shortcomings of the Party; he fully realised that our candidates needed to be better and work harder.

I wasn't the only member of the Party who'd pictured him as the first Labor premier since 1957. Allowed his time, he may even have been premier instead of Wayne Goss. Murphy's assessment had been that Goss would make a very capable attorney-general; that was certainly our plan in earlier days. Denis would have been a visionary premier, someone who would have led an enlightened, tolerant government. It would have been an honour to serve under him. Sadly, that wasn't to be; Denis Murphy died of cancer in June 1984.

Denis's death was a personal blow for me and a setback to the fortunes of Labor. At the 1984 State Conference in Townsville, many were visibly upset, including Terry Hampson, the Party's Assistant Secretary, and me. But two key lessons were reaffirmed for me, namely that politics stops for no one and that grief is very personal. It's a pretty savage reality that political power is a stronger force than sentiment or sympathy.

The Party conference that year was not noted for any picnic or carnival-like atmosphere. The Left's Ian McLean, whom I had defeated three years earlier for the job of state secretary, managed to achieve the presidency. Although he wasn't my preferred candidate, he certainly grew in the role over time and in my opinion became an effective and pragmatic contributor.

Seeking preselection

In the Brisbane City Council election of 1985, when Liberal candidate Sallyanne Atkinson rolled Roy Harvey, Labor was ousted from City Council for the first time since 1961. By then I'd been state secretary for four years. Although I felt I had done a good job, I was ready to move on — I wanted to try to make a difference in the forum that counted most, parliament.

With the death of sitting member John Goleby, the National Party Minister for Irrigation and Water Resources, the opportunity to stand for parliament presented itself. Goleby had held the bay-side seat of Redlands. Three of us put our hands up for ALP preselection for the seat — local Party identity Con Sciacca, a less-known Party member named Ron Pokarier, and me.

My attitude was that I could and would think and act locally — even though I wasn't a local — at the same time as I would think and act state-wide. It was well within my capability to respond to local needs; the key requirement for a candidate, in my view, was to understand and carry the Party's policy state-wide and not become bogged down in factions.

Much as I expected, Sciacca had two-thirds of the numbers in the first stage of preselection, the local vote. I felt I would do better in the second stage of preselection, the Electoral College.

The argument I developed was that, 'for the individual, winning a seat is not an end in itself, it is a means to an end. That end is the election of a Labor government.' That said, then came the tricky part — winning the Electoral College ballot. This was the area where factions and faction numbers could make or break my candidature. To come in ahead of the others, I needed twenty-seven or twenty-eight of the total forty-two votes. What I was banking on was the likelihood that the Socialist Left and Labor Unity (or Old Guard) groups would vote together against Con's faction, the Australian Workers Union–Centre Majority.

Upon arrival at Party headquarters at Breakfast Creek for the crucial meeting, I discovered my educated guesswork to be meaningless. Labor Unity were intending to back Sciacca. No amount of stirring speech was going to swing things my way. Beating Sciacca 21–20, as I did in this Electoral College vote, was not enough. Adding his strong first-stage vote to the twenty he achieved on this occasion gave Con the numbers. Preselection for Redlands was his. Ron Pokarier, who by now had assumed the status of the ghost at the feast, got the single remaining Electoral College vote.

Because I meant what I'd said about the Party being bigger than the individual, I went on to be Con's campaign manager in the ensuing by-election. Neither of us was destined for glory on this occasion, however, as National Party candidate Paul Clauson just managed to get over the line. And it's what happens on the day that really counts.

It is no secret that after this preselection defeat my standing within the Party took a serious blow. I was not well-loved, or even particularly liked, by some Old Guard factional sections and individuals. For a time I did seriously wonder whether there was any point continuing in politics if I was to be blocked by vengeful and negative enemies rather than allowed to work towards a positive future for the Party. Upon reflection, as had been the case with the Reform Group generally, I was already too far down the track.

Abandon the gains we'd made? Give up? These weren't options. With Heather's blessing, I got back into the fray.

The 'gerrymandered' '86 election

There was no great joy for me or the Party when the 1986 state election rolled around. To add to our shortcomings in matters of unity and administration (not to mention negative perceptions of our economic competence) we were about to be wrong-footed by the other side's dirty tricks. Thanks to the electoral redistribution of November 1985, the Labor Party of Queensland went into the 1986 contest the victim of a five-star malapportionment of electoral boundaries.

In the City of Brisbane, the redistribution had the effect of containing metropolitan Labor votes in a few already strong Labor seats. In some country areas, the anomalies were even more apparent and detrimental to Labor. For example, the Indigenous community of Wujal Wujal in North Queensland had been made part of the Cook electorate, even though it was physically located in the Barron River seat next door, so it became an 'island' in an adjoining seat.

Federal factors compounded our woes. The federal ALP introduced some changes to the fringe benefits tax. Even though this impacted a tiny number of privileged individuals, the National Party in Queensland turned this into yet another instance of high-taxing Labor at work.

The hapless Liberals gave the Nationals a leg-up when their leader, Sir William Knox, had something like a divine revelation and announced he would be the next premier of Queensland. This, of course, did not wash with Liberal voters, who switched their support to Joh's party.

The long and short of the 1986 poll was that the National Party under Joh Bjelke-Petersen unfortunately roared back in, winning votes away from the Liberals as well as our side, finishing up with a total of forty-nine seats, and being able to govern all on their own once more.

This result was a major blow to the ALP in Queensland. Much humbled, we went back to the drawing board. Clearly we needed better policies, we needed to improve our campaign techniques, and we needed better leadership.

QUEENSLAND BEFORE AND AFTER FITZGERALD

Our history

No one should look at the basket case that was Queensland politics during the 1980s and assume that it was all Joh's fault. Historically, many Queenslanders had been a conservative agrarian bunch — pioneers who often did it tough dealing with the elements as well as geographic isolation — a small population in a physically large state with no great industrial base and no industrial cities. The cost of reaching this far-flung population with transport and education services was reflected in the relatively low standards of both. Queen and Empire were rallying points. Following the state's proclamation in 1859 as a colony separate from New South Wales, Queenslanders willingly signed up for the wars and shared in all the turmoil and hardship they inevitably brought.

Consider how Federation came about: Brisbane voted against it, worried about the manufacturing southern states swamping Queensland; others, including North Queensland, voted for it because they wanted to get a better go. I've already mentioned the so-called Brisbane Line that was mooted during World War II; what a slap in the face that was.

There's been plenty of groundbreaking activity, too. With the Anderson Dawson government of 1899, Queensland had the first labour government in the world; T. J. Ryan's government of 1915–19 was the first ever majority government. Under Ryan, the state was a model of progressive ideas. It was his government that assisted the struggling sugar farmers of that period, a group not then seen as the 'natural' constituency of Labor.[1] We were also progressive in the early period of the 1920s, under E.G. Theodore. It was Theodore who left Queensland with the considerable blessing of not having an Upper House, when his government managed to legislate away the Legislative Council of that era. That made Queensland the only state in Australia with a one-house parliament and the envy of others.[2]

Despite such stand-outs, a conservatism took hold in Queensland that continued through governments of both persuasions. Queensland has had its share of Labor inertia — the Gair years stand out in that regard. But with all their faults these periods didn't leave as much wreckage, in my view, as the more socially damaging conservatism associated with the National Party and National–Liberal coalitions.

Down the years, only rarely have Queensland voters given a gong to any sort of radical. The celebrated exception is Fred Patterson, who in 1944 became the only communist to have been elected to a state parliament. An open climate? No. Dissent has not exactly been tolerated through Queensland history.

There were corrupt administrations under the Nationals and Liberals and a number of matters that were certainly questionable under Labor governments. Famously in the 1950s we had a split in the Labor Party in Queensland, as elsewhere in Australia. In 1957, Vince Gair was expelled from the Party while he was still premier. With that episode, Labor kissed goodbye to rule in Queensland for the following thirty-two years.

Nice figures but terrible costs

History or no history, it was sickening to witness the negative effects of the National–Liberal coalition government in action during the '60s through '80s. Admittedly, state governments hadn't been funding education appropriately for at least fifty years — facilities were inadequate; money was not spent on maintenance. But the Nationals' practice of building schools mainly in non-Labor-held seats really took the cake.

Other areas had been starved of funding, too. Health was languishing. Government social policy was ad hoc — the lack of commitment to multiculturalism and the lack of tolerance of difference were stridently obvious. Environmental vandalism was rife. You had only to look around to see examples. In the name of development, heritage buildings like the Bellevue Hotel on George Street had been demolished in the middle of the night. Governments didn't seem to care.

However, people outside the state were noticing these things. Queensland had a dodgy reputation. It was positively embarrassing. Perhaps most embarrassing of all, the low point in the story of Queensland, was the woeful policing of crime and the endemic corruption.

Notwithstanding the above, I would be the first to admit that the modern period of conservative rule wasn't all a total disaster. There was some good economic activity and I have given credit in the past to Joh Bjelke-Petersen: guided by two brilliant public servant heads, Sid Schubert and Leo Hielscher, Bjelke-Petersen made a significant contribution to economic development. It is fair to note his achievements there, even while acknowledging the close and allegedly corrupt relationships between developers and the government. However, without Hielscher, Schubert, and Liberal Treasurer Sir Gordon Chalk, this contribution would not have happened.

But from my point of view Bjelke-Petersen denied the sort of openness that is a prerequisite to the creation of a better society. Corruption in the police service, corruption in politics, bribery rife, brown paper bags being flung about, it was just an outrageous situation. To top it off, the politicians in charge in those days had a very autocratic 'don't you worry about that, leave that to me' attitude towards the voters of this state.

A culture of misconduct

As with Queensland conservatism, it is useful to note that the roots of the law enforcement problem ran deep. During the early colonial period policing was undertaken by British soldiers in New South Wales — the infamous Rum Corps. Then ex-convicts were appointed as constables and authorised to exercise corporal punishment among what were, in effect, their peers. By the time colonial governments tried to impose a more ethical approach to policing, the attitude of mutual suspicion between the populace and the police was deeply entrenched.

The use of police and the justice system to support the landed aristocracy in the great strikes of the 1880s and 1890s served to further develop this distrust. When you also had 'wowsers' trying to ban gambling, alcohol and other 'vices', you were creating a recipe for a social problem down the track, especially when the police came from — and generally lived in — the same working-class environments as those they were supposed to keep in line. Some of the by-products of this culture were anti-police creeds — things like it was 'un-Australian' to 'dob' or blow the whistle on those committing crimes or misdeeds.

The events of 1987

By the 1980s police corruption and other forms of institutionalised graft in Queensland had run amok. Why? In order to fight corruption we have to understand its forms as well as origins, and for too long we were unwilling as a society to tackle these questions.

The ALP had dropped the ball. Within the party at the time, there were probably some who felt paralysed — who had convinced themselves that Labor would always lose or that a gerrymander was insurmountable and who, psychologically, may have given up. To be honest, some individuals succumbed to the temptation to be time servers on the Opposition benches, to hold a safe seat but not to actively participate in government. People like Kevin Hooper and Wayne Goss, from 1983, did fight, but it was hard going.

I also believe sections of the media had failed in their duties. They didn't pursue the difficult stories and, if they did touch on them, it was not with anything like the proper energy or commitment. The normal, corrective mechanisms had broken down.

Eventually, the circuit-breaking energy emerged, beginning with gutsy police whistle-blowers and a few maverick journalists. On 12 May 1987, the day after a program by investigative journalist Chris Masters went to air on ABC TV,[3] Deputy Premier and Police Minister Bill Gunn announced an independent and open inquiry. It would come to be known as the Fitzgerald Inquiry.

Joh was away at the time — amusingly enough, in Disneyland. It was clearly a mistake from their political point of view — but their greatest mistakes had already been made, and Queensland had paid the price.

As for Gunn's motivations, I can only speculate. Having interviewed him over a fair period of time for what was originally my PhD thesis, I came to understand him reasonably well. A string of National Party ministers were crooks, but Gunn wasn't. A man with an old country idea about honour, he had reached that stage in his career where he was interested in doing what was right. He may have come to the view that he didn't like what was going on and took the opportunity to do something to remedy it. He might also have been panicked by the media. I like to believe he wanted to do the right thing.

Joh wasn't at all happy about the prospect of parts of his government and administration being held up to scrutiny. With his ministers Don Lane and Russ Hinze, he talked about closing down the Fitzgerald Inquiry. But it was too late. The inquiry was a force of history and would prove to be a catalyst for widespread reform. Once the public realised the extent of the corruption, they were persuaded of the desirability of change.

Fitzgerald and the inquiry

Tony Fitzgerald was underestimated initially. A fiercely independent individual who deserves enormous credit for his work — completed at considerable personal and family cost — his inquiry was a lens through which, finally, people were able to see the seriousness of the corruption. At first, many refused to believe what they were confronting — there is always a degree of cynicism about media and public institutions, after all. But essentially, here was an honest man exposing some big problems.

The Fitzgerald Commission of Inquiry, convened from 1987 to 1989, made it clear that a succession of state governments had superintended corruption over a great many years.[4] It opened up to scrutiny the Licensing Branch — to show what was happening in the form of protection of prostitution and gaming. Then it revealed how corruption existed at all levels. That the Police Commissioner (then 'Sir') Terence Lewis himself accepted bribes was one of the more dramatic revelations. The Queensland Police Force, Commissioner Fitzgerald declared, 'is debilitated by misconduct, inefficiency, incompetence, and deficient leadership'. He continued:

The situation is compounded by poor organisation and administration, inadequate resources, and insufficiently developed techniques and skills for the task of law enforcement in a modern complex society. Lack of discipline, cynicism, disinterest, frustration, anger and low self-esteem are the result. The culture which shares responsibility for, and is supported by, this grossly unsatisfactory situation includes contempt for the criminal justice system, disdain for the law and rejection of its application to police, disregard for the truth, and abuse of authority.[5]

Beyond police mismanagement, the Fitzgerald Commission of Inquiry also looked at the whole system of democracy in the state. The police had become part of an apparatus to thwart democratic activity. For instance, if you chose to protest in a public place you ran the risk of getting bashed. If three people were to stand on a corner or as a group, they were liable to be arrested. Priests couldn't sing in parks. There was a Special Branch that chased people around if they didn't like the look of them, taking photos and spying on them. It was a closed society in the sense that people were only allowed to exercise their rights as citizens by the grace and favour of the police.

Although there had been an electoral gerrymander under Labor from the late 1940s, it was truly perfected by Bjelke-Petersen. In Queensland, an unsavoury culture of 'winner takes all' had crept in. It was in many ways an unpleasant environment. The Fitzgerald Report not only helped to transform policing in Queensland, it also encouraged electoral reform, improved transparency and led to the establishment of an independent anti-corruption body, the Criminal Justice

Commission (CJC). Now named the Crime and Misconduct Commission (CMC), it expects integrity not only in the police but broadly across the public sphere and has the authority to launch investigations.[6]

During part of the inquiry I was a Labor party solicitor, as I had gone back into legal practice with Peter Channel & Associates after retiring as ALP secretary in August 1988. Never will I forget those revelations of corruption, police on the take, people rolling over. My own reaction to the revelations — anger, mixed in with a fair amount of disappointment — wasn't a political response but a concern for Queensland's reputation. These ills had been happening in the place where we all lived, a place I love. The moral inadequacies and the credibility of Queensland were receiving national media coverage.

Once the Fitzgerald Inquiry was underway, there was a sense of 'at last we are going to fix a festering sore'; a sense of 'let's put things right'. No gloating. It would be disingenuous of me to say that there were no political advantages for our side in pursuing the course of exposé and, ultimately, justice. But when the Fitzgerald Inquiry was cracking all these crooks, and they were being punished, I didn't take any great pride in it. Politics is there to make things better; never have I viewed those on the other side as always and completely bad. (Among my friends are members of the Liberal Party — in a democracy they as much as anyone else have the right to be wrong! — and they are good, decent people. I've been friends with Ian Walker, who was on the Liberal Party Council for years, since we were at law school together.) On a human level, I didn't feel great either. These people were the government, the police commissioner, these were the people running the state, and it was quite depressing to see them established as at least dishonest or, at worst, crooks. Queensland was the laughing stock of Australia and I hated that.

Out the other end

The Fitzgerald Inquiry is like a line through the history of Queensland — there is a before and an after. We learnt from it. Not only has unethical political behaviour and corruption been removed in our state but we now have far more accountability. The openness and propriety that exists today has never previously existed in Queensland's history. Politics happens on a new, more tolerant plane. In Joh's day, members couldn't even mix in the dining room of Parliament House — the Nationals and Liberals were segregated from Labor. All that, thankfully, has passed.

In essence, what we've had from Wayne Goss's premiership through to now — with a short interlude of going backwards under Rob Borbidge's interregnum — is a period of growing enlightenment. And I use the word deliberately, with its traditional meaning. We are working to eliminate superstition, ignorance and prejudice, and to promote science and knowledge that will benefit humanity. We have developed a new Labor, new values, new openness, a revolution in Queensland and a more open society. One pleasing outcome of this is the snide remarks about Queensland that used to be very common in Sydney and Melbourne are now heard less often.

My desire to do something for my state's reputation was sharpened by the way things developed through the Joh years. But my sense of wanting to do something, as an individual, for Queensland, had its origins, I am sure, in a great love of the place and its people. That began when I was a young person living up north but developed once I got involved in union work and then politics, and travelled the state.

Queensland, I realised, is a hard place not to love. Things like Brisbane on the river, a walk in the Botanic Gardens on Alice Street, going for a bike ride in the sunshine, the way the jacarandas flower in October and November, the openness and directness of the best sort of Queensland character — these have always made up for some of the less savoury aspects that you might come across. They helped keep me going through the Joh years and through the inquiry. They still do.

LEARNING THE ROPES,

1987-89

Gagged

Before the Fitzgerald Inquiry began in 1987, the ALP was going through changes of its own. By late 1986 I did not have the numbers to remain much longer as state secretary, a circumstance both Denis Murphy and I had foreseen.

Denis and I knew that as the elements who left the party after federal intervention in 1980 rejoined, we would lose the numbers. Our strength lay more in the branch membership than in the unions. However, the factions were cautious in moving against me because of my branch support.

When the Socialist Left and the AWU factions teamed up and then hatched a plan to control the administrative wing of the Party, trouble was just around the corner for me. Using the loss of the Brisbane City Council in 1985 as his pretext, Errol Hodder of the AWU got stuck into me in January 1987. Hodder took the angle that I had 'hogged the media', drawing attention away from those who really mattered — the parliamentary Party. If hogging the media involved getting as much useful exposure for the Party as possible by creating an extensive network of media contacts and by supplying those contacts with positive information on behalf of the Queensland Labor Party, then I was certainly guilty. I failed to see a problem.

Con Sciacca, another AWU member and now a close friend, weighed in with his two cents' worth. He wanted, he said, 'to ensure from henceforth that the available press coverage that is given by the media to the ALP be best used by persons who will derive the most benefit for the Party itself and not for the individual'.[1] Subsequently, the Administrative Committee was summoned for a special meeting, to which a motion was put that I be banned from talking to the media. The motion went against me 15–10.

To me, the gag was essentially meaningless. I resolved that while I was still secretary of the Queensland ALP I would continue to do my job, as I saw it, for the betterment of the Party. The rank and file, both at branch and at individual level, showed me sterling and heartening support, for which I have always been grateful. Whatever else happened, I was determined not to give in to pressure and resign — that would do too much damage and, besides, I was determined to ensure the possibility of an orderly succession.

Fortunately, Nev Warburton, the state parliamentary leader, was able to play a positive part in resolving the impasse. Though he himself was of the Labor Unity (Old Guard) faction and therefore not able to command huge support on the Administrative Committee, through his good offices and a series of meetings over which he presided, the matter progressed somewhat. I was granted a partial lifting of the gag — and I retained my position as state secretary.

1987 federal election

The Nationals' capture of forty-nine seats in the 1986 state election, in the newly enlarged 89-seat parliament, was the best result they had ever had. From that point, Joh began to feel invincible, a bad sign in any human being but a particularly unfortunate one in a politician. Egged along, as always, by some spectacularly misguided supporters, he presumed he could step in and become the nation's saviour. In the run-up to the 1987 federal election he starred in an ill-fated campaign with the hillbilly-sounding title of 'Joh for PM'.

The ALP had its third successive federal win in 1987, the first time that had ever happened. Queensland Labor did well, which was a boon, especially as we lost seats in Victoria and New South Wales. As Queensland's campaign director, I'd found the work of securing additional seats in our state stimulating. We targeted four seats as possible new gains and two others that we already held. In the event, we won all six.

The previously marginal Rankin and Brisbane became more secure; we picked up Petrie, Forde, Fisher and Hinkler — the latter two from the Nationals; plus we managed sizeable swings in Moreton and Dawson. Large swings were recorded against the National Party in their other supposedly safe seats. They responded by going into panic mode.

Once the campaign to install Joh in Canberra failed, further more serious problems arose for him. As 1987 wore on, his own side began to make efforts to dislodge him. In what was to be a last-ditch attempt at showing he was still in charge, he tried to sack five of his Cabinet ministers. This move went down a bit like dropping a match into your own box of fireworks — things start to explode and fly off in all directions. Mike Ahern, whom Joh disliked with a vengeance — perhaps because he was the only National with a degree — was dismissed by his leader on 24 November but gained the leadership of his party the very next day. Still Joh somehow imagined he could hang on as premier.

A meeting with Joh

Not long after the attempted gagging, Queensland politics really hotted up. A businessman with links to the major political parties contacted me. Evidently the beleaguered premier wanted to toss around some ideas with me; Joh's few remaining parliamentary supporters were prepared to cross the floor and join the Labor and Liberal parties. What Joh wanted to do was to stay in power.

Meanwhile, what topped Labor's wish-list was a one vote, one value, fair electoral redistribution.

After calculating the many and serious risks involved, I phoned the by now less-than-venerable Sir Joh Bjelke-Petersen. I had nothing to lose. My time as ALP secretary was running out. After listening to him vent some spleen about Ahern and the National Party President, Sir Robert Sparkes, I outlined my position, explaining that I would not put to my party any such idea as he was suggesting unless there was a positive return, namely a fair and equitable redistribution of seats to end the gerrymander and give the ALP an equal chance at the next election. I also told him that deciding on any subsequent course of action would not be undertaken by me and me alone.

Over the next two days I wrestled privately with what we'd discussed, and all that it could mean. I spoke to the State President, Ian McLean, and to the Federal Secretary, Bob McMullan. Via the businessman who had first contacted me on this matter, I also met with Sir Edward Lyons, one of Bjelke-Petersen's most solid supporters. All he could tell me was that he had told Joh not to resign — a meaningless injunction, I thought, given that the man had already been 'run out'. He then made the suggestion that I meet with Sir Joh face-to-face. I agreed.

A meeting was arranged to take place, not in Brisbane where we would easily be spotted, but at Bethany, the Bjelke-Petersen property at Kingaroy. We met there one afternoon, in a field on his holding not obvious to any prying eyes. Bjelke-Petersen sat in the back of my car while I sat in the front. Then he laid out what he had to offer. If we were to support him, he would give the ALP more staff and facilities, he said. He would also agree not to proceed with the eight defamation actions he had underway against people in the ALP. But on the truly important matter of a fair redistribution, he had nothing positive to say. Indeed, he mumbled and muttered for a time, only to end up being entirely non-committal. And that, from my point of view, was that. The 'plot', such as it might have been, was no more; it would never get off the ground.

A few pleasantries were then exchanged, but when the premier tried to get out of my car, he found the doors wouldn't budge — child locks had been fitted. (Oh the beauty of being a father of three young children.) As I got out and came around to his side, he looked distinctly worried. Perhaps he thought he was to be kidnapped and held to ransom by the Labor Party?

As for Joh, the inevitable finally happened and he called me at my home, on 1 December 1987, to tell me that he was finished. Frankly, that was something I was glad to hear. With his removal came the close of his long involvement in the state's political affairs and nineteen years as premier. More than anything, Joh had become the victim of his own hubris.

Now I shake my head when I look back on my preparedness to run a spoiling game. I'd contemplated obtaining fairer electoral boundaries via a temporary arrangement on the floor of parliament, all in the interest of destabilising a ruling party that the Labor Party considered 'the enemy'. I would no longer advocate such a style of politics or political activity for myself or others. Still, even if from today's perspective it was more about what not to do, that episode was all part of my learning and growing up politically.

Wayne Goss becomes leader

In March 1988, Nev Warburton honourably agreed to stand aside as leader of the Party in Queensland after continued negative polling on his electoral chances. After some complex negotiations, Wayne Goss replaced him as leader. Warburton's dignified departure was a credit to him. He had given good service to the Party and was a member of the strongest parliamentary faction at the time, Labor Unity. To the voters, these things meant little. Goss was seen as fresh and competent, and was liked and trusted in the electorate. He was the most prominent member of the new blood that had come into parliament after the reform of the Party, along with David Hamill, Pat Comben and, early on, Denis Murphy.

The year 1989 saw Labor solidly behind Wayne Goss. As an independent within the Party, he was able to win cross-factional support so that ours was the best Opposition the Party had put up in a long time. For a whole generation, we had not really presented ourselves as a credible, inspiring alternative government. And when all was said and done, that was the real reason Labor kept being rejected by the electorate.

Politically, a few cards had also fallen in our favour. Joh had departed and, though Premier Ahern was a good man, the Fitzgerald Inquiry had been underway for some time with continual revelations of the breadth and depth of corruption within the National Party government and its public administration.[2] A couple of months ahead of the election, which was called for 2 December, the Nationals made the first in a series of blunders in tactics and strategy. They changed leaders, replacing Mike Ahern with police minister Russell Cooper. The problem was that Cooper came across more as a force for instability than anything else — he had, after all, tried to oust Ahern three months earlier.

The Nationals then went on to run a reactive, negative election campaign, something you see quite often when governments have run out of policy ideas and energy. Some of the usual fear tactics were trotted out — they tried, among other things, to suggest Labor would bring about the moral collapse of society.

Gaining preselection

The way I look at it, if you are Party secretary and leave the role still popular with everyone, it probably means you've been a failure. Since taking up the position just under seven years earlier, I had tried to find and present good candidates, and I had tried to modernise the Party for the better. I'd brought in direct mail, phone campaigning and targeted research — all techniques which I'd observed on political exchange visits to Britain and the United States. As a result of these innovations, I had drawn a level of personal animosity from people who understood the old ways better than the new.

When I ran for preselection in 1988, I was opposed by all the factions. There was a 60 per cent rule at the time, which meant that if you obtained 60 per cent or more of the local vote it didn't go to the Central College. Thanks to my strong local support, I ended up with 71 per cent. Had that not been the case, I would have been knocked off by the factions and never heard from again.

My support has always come from ordinary rank and file membership of the Party, built on the fact that I've worked locally and am well known in my area. As Party secretary, I had consistently argued for rank and file rights against the political machinery. And I'd been identified with Denis Murphy and the Reform Movement — that is, with the democratisation of the Labor Party.

During the preselection process, the opposition to me inside the Party was unequivocal. A few individuals across different factions did support me, but I had people campaigning against me and trying to encourage people to run against me, both from the Left and the Right.

My luck held. Brian Davis, the Labor member for Brisbane Central, was retiring. In the end I was able to stand for that seat, which had long been held by Labor.

Brisbane Central

The seat of Brisbane Central used to go across the Brisbane River to South Bank; now it runs back north of the river. It had been lost to Labor only briefly in the 1970s, in the backlash vote against Whitlam.

I never took anything for granted in my bid for a seat in parliament. I worked hard, door-knocked, distributed a calendar, did as much grassroots work as possible. I campaigned on a number of local issues, in particular roads, public housing, education and health. I also campaigned against the development of Hale Street, a council road ruining one of my suburbs. My campaign focused on a range of specific issues, but it was also as broadly based as possible, covering the areas that we felt had been neglected but which very much mattered to voters.

The election day result made it all worthwhile.

UNDERWAY AT LAST, 1989-95

Victory

The Goss victory of 2 December 1989 was a great day for the people of Queensland and for the ALP. It was the first time the ALP had been in power in Queensland in thirty-two years. That Saturday was also the day I was first elected to parliament.

A string of National Party ministers lost their seats. To be blunt, it was a satisfying spectacle for me. They had been there too long and had clearly stopped serving any publicly useful purpose. With 50.3 per cent of the first preference vote we ended up winning fifty-four of the eighty-nine seats in the Legislative Assembly, the Nationals winding up with twenty-seven, and the Liberals eight.[1]

It was a wonderful experience — exhilarating even. 'Come around afterwards,' I said to a few people and ended up with something like five hundred guests at my place till about five in the morning. We had everybody you could think of there — having been a Party secretary, a lot of Party workers came along as well as the local rank and file.

But the euphoria to one side, I was soon thinking, 'Where do we go next?' 'What are we going to do?'

Like everybody else on our side, I was thrilled that we had a Labor government at long last. The prospects and opportunities ahead were exciting, and I wanted to work hard for my electorate and constituency.

Wayne and me — setting the record straight

My relationship with Wayne Goss has been a subject of conjecture for some, over the years. A little background might help put the speculation at rest. Along with Denis Murphy, I was one of the people who encouraged Wayne to run for the seat of Salisbury then fostered the deal that supported him. We needed people like Wayne Goss. So back in the early 1980s, '82 more accurately, I supported Wayne for the '83 election. In him I recognised a good leader, someone who could take the Labor Party into office. Which is what he did.

The Labor Party in Queensland had been through a long period where we had difficulties putting to the electorate a credible leadership team or leader who would win their support. Wayne was good at that and, not to be too modest, with my solid campaign management background, I thought I was as well.

Allowing for the obvious — that the Labor Party had two potential leaders and therefore there was always going to be an element of creative tension between us — I don't believe we ever had as bad a relationship as some might have imagined. He came along to my place to celebrate on the night that I won my preselection for the seat of Brisbane Central. It should also be understood that some of Wayne's trusted supporters were always nervous about me.

I thought Wayne was a very good premier. Even if he made mistakes and went out of office, he made a tremendous contribution to the state. Although Wayne was premier ahead of me, he had my support. My ambition in that regard has been often misunderstood. What I always wanted, first and foremost, was to see a Labor government in office.

If the Labor Party had, in effect, two leaders — one the premier, and the other to whom some sections of the Party tended to look for leadership — the electorate would later resolve that difficulty. Through that period I did have a strained relationship with Wayne Goss — manoeuvrings of factional players and particularly their desire to exclude me were key factors in that. Over time, our relationship improved dramatically; these days we get on well.

New kid on the block

Life as a new MP had its challenges. The parliament itself works in peculiar ways. We have our own unique spin on the Westminster system; sometimes it seems like a beast with a mind of its own. At first the Standing Orders — a strange, antiquated breed of rules — were like Egyptian hieroglyphics; they've since been improved. When you get up to speak, the other side wants you to fall flat on your face. And they're not the only ones — some of your own side do, too. Not now of course, but this was the story in the early '90s. It can be a testing time for any new MP, and I must admit to experiencing my share of nerves. I took things cautiously and slowly.

As a local member there were various projects that were important to me, particularly improving educational opportunities. In my electorate, it was important to develop schooling for the disabled, to update schools and see that they were properly funded; they had been the victims of National Party prejudice for years. Electoral work was enjoyable for numerous reasons, not least for the personal contact I was able to have with people.

During my first term in parliament, I also had to work out how to operate in the legislative arena. In order to make thoughtful contributions to legislation, and not wishing to make a goose of myself, I had to figure out how to properly research contributions to legislation — my legal training certainly came in handy. I purposely spoke on a whole range of bills covering a variety of matters in order to force myself to learn across portfolios. By taking an interest in areas in which I hadn't previously had experience, I was seeking to broaden my understanding.

As some people have suggested occasionally, I am a driven person. I believe passionately in what I do. I don't believe in doing things in a half-hearted way. I'm determined — yes, I'm even feisty — but I'm not a hater and I don't carry grudges. Once an argument is over, then it's over. If I'm wrong or make a mistake, I admit it, fix the problem and move on. Life is too short to agonise over yesterday's drama. But I'm also compassionate, with a compassion driven by the Australian principle of a fair go.

The experience of being in parliament was something I came to enjoy, even love. As someone committed to the democratic process, even now I find parliament a stimulating place to be. I love Question Time. It's the most fun I'm allowed to have as premier.

The Parliamentary Criminal Justice Committee

I was honoured when Wayne Goss offered me the chair of one of the two major Fitzgerald committees, the Parliamentary Criminal Justice Committee (the PCJC) — the chair of the Parliamentary Committee for Electoral and Administrative Review (PCEAR) went to Matt Foley. The opportunity to achieve reform in Queensland through one of the major bodies overseeing the Criminal Justice Commission, as it was then, was right on target with my ambitions and aspirations. I wanted to be effective, to help form a good Labor government and to ensure that the Fitzgerald reforms worked. Let me stress that, as a newcomer to parliament, I knew deep down that it would have been unreasonable to expect a ministry during my first term, much as I would have loved it.

Nothing like the PCJC had ever existed before, and I was its first chair. Set up by an Act of Parliament, it was designed by Tony Fitzgerald to monitor the powerful new body rapidly gaining importance as the public's watchdog. Fitzgerald had not wanted a minister to be in a position to interfere in the running of the CJC and opted instead for a bipartisan committee to hold it accountable. There were seven of us — four Labor members and three conservatives. The Labor members were Wendy Edmond, later to become my health minister from June 1998 until the 2004 election; Robert Schwarten, later Minister of Public Works, Housing and Racing; and Margaret Woodgate, who was later in my shadow ministry until forced out by ill health after a short while. The first deputy chair was Mike Ahern. Bill Gunn, who had been deputy premier under Joh and Ahern, and who, of course, appointed the Fitzgerald Commission, replaced Ahern when he resigned from parliament. Neville Harper, the Attorney-General under Joh, made up the second National Party representative. The other conservative was Liberal Santo Santoro.

Not only were these committees bipartisan in make-up, many of the decisions required the support of more than one political party. This had never happened before. It was also in the days when there were no independents in parliament.

Up until then, the parliamentary committee system had been utterly toothless. The only, mild, precedent for what we were launching into had been a Public Accounts Committee, which had been extremely limited in what it could achieve; its powers have since been broadened. Having been a solicitor at the Fitzgerald Inquiry I believed wholeheartedly in the inquiry and its reforms, and still do. Matt Foley and I both put in an enormous amount of effort to see that the committee system worked.

Every month, we met with the CJC; they accounted to us for what they were doing and reported on operational matters when they were completed. The workload was enormous. We were charting new territory and there weren't that many maps. Plus I was still getting the hang of being in parliament — it was something of a baptism of fire.

Being part of the team involved in the successful establishment of the PCJC is among the highlights of my entire parliamentary career. We operated it in a way that was honest and fair. If we had not done that then the slipping and sliding would doubtless have started. You've got to have some way to keep the bastards honest; that may have been a favourite line of the Democrats but, practically, that's what the CJC does. It's kept Queensland honest and it's now well established. Today, as premier, I am the Minister for the Crime and Misconduct Commission (CMC) as it's now called, but I'm only responsible for budgetary matters. The Commission is still kept accountable by a parliamentary committee.

Prostitution, an eye-opener

Prominent among the issues which the PCJC examined was prostitution. We spent time researching the matter in Sydney and Melbourne and to a degree in Adelaide and Perth, and we talked with many sex workers.

It was extraordinary for a country boy like me to be going around the country studying various brothels and their practices. Committee members Bill Gunn and Robert Schwarten, in particular, used to lighten things up from time to time with a little humour. Once we happened to be in Perth at the same time as a visiting US warship. Some of the W.A. police were looking after us, and they took us to look at a nearby brothel. While we were sitting there having a discussion with the madam, one of the young women went by. I can't remember exactly who it was, but one of the Committee members said something like, 'Crikey, there can't be any money in this — they can't afford any clothes!' Bill Gunn always had a wonderful sense of humour and it may indeed have been him who said it.

More seriously, I discovered that prostitution is not a straightforward story. There is a common belief, for instance, that most if not all women who go into prostitution do it to support a drug habit. And yet there are very many women who aren't on drugs and who go into the industry for all sorts of reasons. Among them are single parents who need to support a child or children. Others are pragmatic types with a view to making a quick quid and then getting out — some claim that this kind of participant represents the majority, although that is not my view. I met many who became prostitutes thinking they would do that kind of work for a while then get out, but didn't. Most stunning to me was the number of people I ran into who had normal jobs during the day and who worked at prostitution by night. One girl I spoke to in Sydney held a job with a major financial insurance company and moonlighted as a prostitute.

Being presented with these and other realities gave me a lot of perspective I had previously lacked. For clients who are unable to get gratification anywhere else, the prostitutes insisted they are really more like counsellors than sex workers. My ideas about the meaning of terms such as 'victim' were shaken up. In many cases, 'the exploited' is a better term.

In terms of the bigger picture, everything we saw confirmed the linkages between political and police corruption and prostitution. It all pointed to the need to have checks and balances in place, and I concluded that society would be better off if prostitution-related offences were decriminalised. However, I wasn't able to carry that into a majority on my committee and we split four–three. Santo Santoro, Wendy and

I voted for, and Robert Schwarten, Margaret Woodgate and the two Nationals voted against.

Grasping the nettle

In the broader community, reforming the laws relating to issues like prostitution and homosexuality didn't go down well. But these matters were on the agenda as set by Tony Fitzgerald, and we had to deal with them. Their time in the too-hard basket was finally up. Previous governments may have shirked their responsibilities in these areas, but we were prepared to tackle them.

Another thorny issue, one where I lost a lot of standing among my colleagues, was parliamentary travel, which was widely seen as open to abuse. Not everyone understood the Fitzgerald Report, its recommendations or how it was to work; some felt that I should have intervened and stopped the CJC investigating parliamentary travel. There were cases where MPs had gone to places like the snowfields for what were described as study tours — and it was hard for them to justify doing that more than once. And while I believe in travel to broaden members' experience in life, this has to be done professionally and not in the spirit of a perk, even a supposedly justifiable perk. If you are spending public money there has to be some public benefit that flows from such exercises. Had the parliamentary committee tried to stop the CJC from investigating the members' travel, then the whole process would have collapsed. Not only would it have been the wrong thing to do morally, it would have destroyed the whole Fitzgerald reform agenda. And it would have done incredible damage to the Goss government. In the end, a number of government members, including two ministers, resigned as a result of the CJC's report.

Of course the CJC committee also put the cleaners through some of my colleagues over the electoral rorts in 2000. Shortly before the 2001 election, an inquiry revealed that a number of Labor MPs and party activists had been falsely enrolling people to boost the strength of their factions in internal Party ballots. My response was to force from politics all those who were found guilty. If people were rorting the system, what other course of action could there be? I paid a price, too, but it was one worth paying.

Getting back to the early 1990s, it was difficult balancing the interests of electorate, caucus and Party. Once again I found I was Mr Unpopular. There were people who were extremely angry with me, though I had no overt threats. What happens in those instances where people disagree with you on a particular matter is that they will rarely put it to you plainly and say they will no longer support you. But then things are said and whispered and done quietly when you are not around. Sadly, that's the nature of politics. At one stage I wouldn't have had more than two votes in caucus, and one of those was my own!

Should I have just been looking after the Labor Party and the government's interests instead of actually being chair of the parliamentary committee with the job of implementing the Fitzgerald reforms? Not on your nelly. The Fitzgerald Inquiry had found corruption among politicians, among government, among police, among every layer of society, including the upper echelons. What was needed in response was a degree of integrity and honesty about what should be done, and it could not be done on a party-political basis.

THE ROAD TO PREMIER,
1996-98

The year 1996 began with the ALP still in power in Queensland — but with a tenuous one-seat majority following the July 1995 state election. By this stage I was serving as Health Minister, but the Goss government itself was ailing. By February 1996, we were in an unfortunately weak and unsustainable position regarding confidence and Supply. The Labor government finally lost power after the Liberals won a crucial by-election in the electorate of Mundingburra, followed by the pledge by Liz Cunningham, conservative Independent member for Gladstone, to support a minority coalition government led by National Party leader Rob Borbidge.

In parliament the Borbidge government had forty-four seats plus the support of Cunningham. Although numerically we looked as though we were within cooee of them with our forty-four seats, in reality our support in the community was running at about half that. A news poll conducted between April and June 1996 gave the Coalition 52 per cent and the ALP 40 per cent.

One thing I will never understand is why the National and Liberal parties didn't ram home their political advantage after forming minority government. As to why Premier Borbidge didn't call a general election as soon as possible after Liz Cunningham gave him her support, I can only speculate. Having waited so long to get there, perhaps he didn't have the nerve to rattle the cage and overturn the expected timing of the election. Perhaps it had to do with a fear that it might upset Liz Cunningham, as she had only just been elected as an independent in July 1995; we tried to persuade her with our argument against an early election. Or did we startle Borbidge when we put the wood on him on that issue? Beyond that, it's possible the Governor, Leneen Ford, may not have granted him an election, may not have allowed him to go to the polls. Whatever the reason, Rob Borbidge missed a golden opportunity as I am convinced he would have wiped us out and kept us out of power until at least 2001.

Getting stuck in

Pessimism was rampant within the Party. It is my belief that certain people only accepted that I was going to become the leader because they thought there would be a long period in Opposition. Even the hard heads and factional leaders thought we had Buckley's chance of winning back government at the forthcoming election, due in 1998. According to conventional wisdom, the electorate gives most governments two terms. The third one tends to be truly ugly, after which it becomes almost impossible to be re-elected for a fourth term — or so it's said.

To come back after one election? No mug punter would back you on that one. The last Queensland government that was defeated after only one term was the Moore government of 1929 to 1932; it was the Depression that knocked it over, in the main. Labor went out of office in 1929 and then came back in with Premier Forgan Smith in 1932. In other words, it had been sixty-six years since anybody had defeated a government after one term. Perhaps the pessimism was understandable, but I didn't pause to analyse it. As the leader of the Labor Party, I had work to do. We simply had to perform. I wasn't going to miss this chance.

In our favour, we had a formidable Opposition front bench. I brought in some fresh blood and, with that touch of rejuvenation, the new team performed extremely well. We worked as a tactical group, leveraging our blend of experience — in people like long-serving ministers Terry Mackenroth and Jim Elder — and new people, such as the energetic and bright Anna Bligh. Our approach was that the shadow Cabinet should act as a real Cabinet. We got stuck into policy development, and soon we were working like a well-oiled policy machine. Everyone was giving 101 per cent.

For at least the first eighteen months, just about the only people who believed that we had a chance of winning an election were my shadow ministers and myself. To their credit, everyone on the Labor side, by and large, wanted to give us a go. Many who would normally have involved themselves in Party manoeuvrings and machinations were prepared to give us a wide berth because they recognised the importance of giving something and someone a chance. Nevertheless, deep down, few believed we could win.

A floundering Coalition

My perception is that the Nats and the Libs, who had become the government, weren't ready for government. They went on to prove they were incompetent in every sense of the word. Although nice enough as private individuals, the Borbidge–Sheldon government wasn't too flash as elected ministers with the responsibilities of public office, and that's putting it mildly.

They were great procrastinators. Within seventy days of taking office in 1996, they had initiated sixty-two reviews.[1] And that figure kept rising. Making decisions may not have been their forte but they did manage to spend a fortune on reviews and inquiries. Keeping a tally of the number of reviews, reports and inquiries they tried to set up became one of our tactics. They also seemed to bring back Dad's Army into the public service; some of their appointments were poor choices and not all government departments were being well run. On the economy, the Coalition tried to do things that made no sense — Disneyland on the Gold Coast, for instance — and proposals that simply couldn't be substantiated.

Whereas we developed a manifesto, a real program which we were to implement when we were eventually voted in, the Coalition had no strategic or policy direction. We were able to effectively expose that shortcoming to the public. Clearly they hadn't done enough policy homework during their time in Opposition. Now that we were the Opposition, we gave them hell. Every angle available to us, we played. In parliament, for instance, we used no confidence motions, we asked penetrating questions, and keenly debated Bills, using that forum as best we could to maintain the pressure on what was a shaky government. The experience of some of our number who had previously been ministers helped us to outmanoeuvre the government. Tacticians like Terry Mackenroth understood the parliament extremely well and were vastly more effective in the Legislative Assembly than were the government ministers.

Not long after I became Opposition Leader in 1996, it was discovered that just before the Mundingburra by-election, the Coalition had entered into a secret deal with the Police Union. This took the form of a Memorandum of Understanding, signed by Police Minister Russell Cooper and Police Union President Gary Wilkinson, in which the Police Union was urging an emasculation of the independent watchdog, the CJC, a weakening of misconduct provisions against its members, and in effect the government giving up the right to choose the police commissioner! The CJC described this agreement as seeking 'to limit the CJC's powers, functions and responsibilities'.[2] Labor tried to bring this deal out into the open by asking for parliament to be recalled for a full debate, but the government refused point blank. Police Minister Russell Cooper was forced into writing to the CJC to ask for an investigation. The CJC then took the course of holding a public inquiry.

Further on, the ALP's fortunes were undoubtedly aided when the Borbidge government tried, as we told parliament, to torpedo some of the Fitzgerald reforms. This was done by attempting to undermine the Carruthers Inquiry, the purpose of which had been to determine if criminal offences or misconduct had taken place in the secret Memorandum of Understanding that had been signed by the National Party before the Mundingburra by-election. The Carruthers Inquiry was eventually told there was enough evidence to consider that a criminal charge of electoral bribery be laid.[3]

In the event, the tainted exercise rebounded most severely on the government. In the parliament in August 1997, we put up a motion of no confidence against the Attorney-General, Denver Beanland, and it was carried.[4] He chose not to resign, and while he continued to stay put, Matt Foley, our shadow Attorney-General, continued to remind the House how many days it had been since the parliament had said it had no confidence in the Attorney-General. Ultimately, the Coalition's stratagems went nowhere, and when it was perceived that the government was trying to wind back reform, Rob Borbidge lost support in the cities.

'100 Days' on the road

In non-metropolitan areas there had been lingering anger with the Goss government, probably because of proposed rail closures and courthouse closures. Our demise in 1996 is attributable to such economically rational measures, decisions that had appeared logical in terms of national competition reform and 'the bottom line' but which went down like a pricked balloon with the electorate. The lesson from that is that Queensland is a community, not a corporation. When Borbidge came in, the regions and the bush were prepared to give him a go. But when he and his government underperformed, there followed an increase in disenchantment: voters were unhappy with politics and politicians across the board, and the potential for a protest vote against both major parties now emerged.

It was at the March 1996 election that Paul Keating lost power — one of the reasons he was defeated that year was that he was unpopular in the regions. That election also saw the ultra-conservative Pauline Hanson, former fish and chip vendor and co-founder of the One Nation Party, voted into federal parliament in the Queensland seat of Oxley. In my assessment, that result was more a fluke than anything else, highly dependent on emotional reactions and anti-Keating sentiment. After all, Oxley had been held by Labor.

Early on in Opposition, we announced that we would travel all over Queensland to listen to what the people were saying. In the process of doing precisely that, we also admitted we'd made mistakes and listened to try to get it right. We knew people had lost faith in politicians and we had to try and come up with the policies that reflected the regions. We travelled the state, slugging away.

That process of listening was to inform the later idea of Community Cabinets, which came out of the discussions I would eventually have with Independent Peter Wellington. Community Cabinets involved the Cabinet spending two days in a particular town or region. Day one was a public meeting where anyone could come along and speak directly with ministers and heads of departments. Day two was the formal Cabinet meeting and an informal lunch with community leaders.

State Conference 1996

Following on from our '100 Days' on the road, we had to debrief the Party itself. At the State Conference of the Queensland ALP in June 1996, I tried to rally the troops, to show them that a win at the next election was within our reach. I explained how the Coalition was trying to return to the bad old days and was thus already reeling; contrasted their policy absence and indecision with our policy committees and drive in this area; and reminded them that the parliamentary scoreboard was 44–44–1. I emphasised that we were only 'a heartbeat away from government'.[5]

The State Conference of 1996 was a turning point. The mood within the Party lifted, behaviour was good, there was a refreshing absence of grandstanding, and those in the factions who tended to like a bit of biff gave it a rest. Media and television coverage was also favourable. That positive meeting was a further sign that we were on the way back, a fact that was noticed by commentators at the time.[6]

Through 1996–97, the ALP in Queensland was rebuilding everywhere. It was clear that those ordinary Labor branch members and uncommitted voters who had become fairly disillusioned wanted a Party that would learn from its mistakes, that had a vision for the future and a strategy to go with it. And that was what we now began to offer. Not only that, we created a prospect of opportunities.

The feeling in Brisbane moved our way because of our opposition to One Nation. The Liberal Party and the National Party would discover in the lead-up to the '98 election that their preparedness to compromise and do deals with One Nation was a bad idea. I believe people wanted politicians and parties who had the courage to stand up — and we did.

I should point out that not everything in the recent past had been a disaster for the Party or perceived as such; we had at least some credit with the electorate from the Goss years. For instance, with the Labor Party's embracing of Fitzgerald reforms, the credibility of the police had dramatically improved.

The rise of Pauline Hanson

Unhappily, 1997 saw Pauline Hanson constantly in the media spotlight. Some commentators saw Hanson as striking a chord with many Australians with her anti-Aboriginal, anti-multiculturalism views, and she soon had a significant following. But from that inauspicious beginning in Oxley, at a time when we had disenchantment with federal Labor and increasing state disenchantment, One Nation started to emerge. Much of the voting public seemed to be saying, look, we've given both the major parties a go and neither of them has been any good. The voters were sick of all of us. Many people in Queensland didn't understand One Nation. Yes, there were a lot of bigots and racists who supported them, but in my view there was more going on with One Nation than purely bigotry and racism. The vote for that group — it never really met the criteria for a formal political party — was largely a response to social dislocation and disenchantment with the major political parties.

My response to the threat she represented at the time was that people should debate with her rationally and expose her 'policies', not guarantee her more media opportunities by demonstrating or attacking her personally. I was concerned that the media was being shallow and fickle, only focusing on the superficial Pauline Hanson; they weren't dealing with the real issues of policy.

When you did get down to dealing with her policies, you saw them for what they were — a joke. Some were anti-Australia, in that they were anti-trade, anti-exports and anti-industry, while others — such as her idea for low-interest loans — were plain ridiculous. They would bankrupt Australia. There was no proper economic thought behind them whatsoever.

Yet, as absurd and laughable as Pauline Hanson's ideas were, she'd managed to convince a whole lot of people who were disenchanted with the major parties — for a whole range of reasons — to lend her their support. But I knew that support was based on emotion rather than substance.

A credible alternative

Throughout 1997 we acted as an alternative government and not just an Opposition. We released ALP policies in all the important areas, beginning as early as January with a promise to restore health funding to previous Labor government levels. We followed with 'New Directions Statements' on such issues as economic and trade development, including a promise to create a new super department (the Department of State Development) and a $2000 incentive to employers for each new apprentice in trades with a shortage of qualified tradesmen. We also promised to provide more police on the beat in trouble spots; and millions more in funds to help the needs of people with disabilities.

As it was really hard to get our policies up in the media, we used the mail; we wrote letters and posted them to every opinion leader in each area of policy. Letters were also sent to the industry bodies, to community groups, academics — all the relevant individuals. We had a hefty postage bill!

Towards the end of 1997, the general perception had developed that we were a credible alternative government. This was reflected in polls. On a two-party preferred basis, 53 per cent of respondents favoured the ALP to win. Nevertheless, having just been belted so badly, we didn't want to indulge in any sort of overconfidence. Besides, the overall political climate was highly uncertain.

At odds with the feds

The year 1998 did not get off to a great start politically. Early on we made known to our federal ALP colleagues that Queensland had some questions that needed to be resolved in relation to Wik Native Title legislation. Borbidge then spent an awful lot of time, effort and taxpayers' money trying to tell people that their backyards were under threat of being taken away from them. In the end, no one believed him. We had a couple of difficult moments over the native title regime that ultimately went through the Senate in Canberra, but while Kim Beazley and I might have disagreed on some of the detail, he and the federal government ultimately delivered an outcome.

On the question of a republic, the other major national issue of that year, my personal view also differed from those of some of my national ALP friends. I supported the Irish model, meaning I supported the direct election of the president. Australians are not going to trust politicians at the end of the day to appoint the President; they want to have a say. In my view, they will only vote for a republic if they can elect the president. I'm sorry Gough; you're wrong!

Campaign focus

In the campaign for the 1998 election we had to overcome extreme voter cynicism. We had been in power less than three years previously and had been found wanting. We stressed Labor's core values — such as the opportunity for all children to reach their full potential through education, for all Queenslanders to have access to first-class health services, and for jobs, jobs, jobs.

Our campaign title was 'Let's Get Queensland Moving Again'. Our major focus was on jobs and we published a critical statement called 'Job Security for Queensland Workers'.[7] The detail covered all the areas that needed serious attention, and proposed solutions such as: partnerships between government and those industry sectors best placed to add value to Queensland's resources; regional development strategies; a comprehensive land use and infrastructure plan to ensure transport, water, energy and other facilities would be provided in a timely and efficient manner; streamlining of regulations to ensure that government did not add to the administrative burden of business; tax reform, by taking part in the national tax reform debate to ensure the workability for Queensland of any new system; strengthening ties with our trading partners; creating a Department of State Development; helping Queensland to grow through a renewal of enterprise development funding grants to business and industry; the implementation of a tourism rescue plan; breaking the unemployment cycle via a massive increase in apprenticeships and traineeships, and new programs to put those facing long-term unemployment to work on essential public works projects; a review of the Competition Principles Agreement with a stronger public benefits test so as to reduce negative employment and social impacts in industry restructuring; and a new and progressive, tripartite system of industrial relations to reduce levels of disputation and ensure that improvements in productivity and workplace efficiencies would not be achieved at the expense of workers.

Going into the closing days of the June election campaign, I felt that we had shown good discipline and gained serious ground. Our policies were striking a chord with the electorate. However, at the end of the campaign we were derailed a little by One Nation and the preference deal they struck with the Nationals.

Our own rejection of One Nation preferences was a decision made on principle. Following my insistence, the Administrative Committee of the Queensland ALP formally decided that One Nation candidates would be placed last on all Labor how-to-vote cards.[8] A couple of people suggested it could cost us, and my response was you don't compromise on this issue; this is about our future as Australians.

Taking that stand did have some tough repercussions. Nevertheless, if I had my time over again I wouldn't act any differently.

1998 election

Finally it was 13 June 1998 and the poll itself; time to face the music. On the night, thanks to an organisational boo-boo of the highest order, trying to find our way into the tally room turned out to be ludicrously difficult. That unsettling experience did nothing to dispel my feelings of pessimism. Instead, they mounted! Towards the end of the evening it looked as though the National Party might be able to hang on in a wild arrangement with the eleven One Nation members who had just been elected. Then the talk turned to the likely new member for Nicklin, a true Independent who would not necessarily support the conservatives even though Nicklin had been viewed as a safe Nationals seat. So I phoned this fellow, Peter Wellington, and said, 'Look, I know it's early, but if you do win in Nicklin and you're interested, I'm happy to talk to you.'

I came away feeling that it wouldn't be easy for anyone to win over Peter Wellington and tried to put that all out of my mind. What was capturing my attention was the thought that after such utter slog, we were going to miss out by a hair's breadth. Politics is many things, but being fair is not one of them.

Throughout two weeks of counting from 13 to 26 June, bit by bit things fell into place for us. It became apparent that we would get forty-four seats. Please, just one more, I kept thinking. We needed forty-five to govern. It was a wild ride. Exasperation followed by rejoicing, and then more hand-wringing.

Between February 1996 and June 1998, Queenslanders had put up with a minority government that couldn't deliver. And now this! To cut a long story short, Peter Wellington turned out to be a fair dinkum bloke. He spoke to all party leaders, including Borbidge and Watson, the Queensland Liberal leader, and eventually he supported us on Supply and motions of no confidence.

First we went through his concerns, one of the main ones being his need to engage the community. Ultimately, that interest of his led to Community Cabinets. When he rang me and said he'd support us, I said I would confirm in writing all the material we'd worked on, which I did out of my electoral office after first conferring with Jim Elder and Terry Mackenroth.

Liz Cunningham then also indicated her support for my government. That surprised a lot people. Rather than being inclined by nature to Labor, she was always naturally more comfortable with the politics of the National Party. By comparison, Wellington was not a Labor person in disguise, but someone I believe is a genuine Independent, a rare phenomenon. I've observed a heck of a lot of politicians masquerading as independents; Peter wasn't one of them. A person of extraordinary integrity, he was primarily interested in his electorate and not himself.

Even though the time has long passed when we needed his support to govern, I have continued to work with him and enjoy doing so. I still find Peter Wellington to be a very impressive individual. He is almost too nice to be a politician!

We're there

After such a long and drawn-out process, the realisation that we'd gained government crept up on us all. After the two years, four months and one week of Coalition government we were able to again form a Labor government.

I announced that we would govern as if we had a majority of ten, and, ultimately, we did do that.

Heather was driving the kids somewhere when she heard Rob Borbidge on radio announce his resignation. It was hardly ideal that she heard the news on the radio first, but my efforts at contacting her had been to no avail. Typically down-to-earth, she remarked to the children, 'I hope you're listening to this because this will be Dad one day.'

She was dead right. Political success never lasts forever. It's an honour to do the job, for even a short period of time, but inevitably the day will come when you have to step down. An attitude of realism reigned at our home. That was in keeping with our policy of trying to shield the children as much as possible from the more bruising side of politics and to lead as normal a life as possible.

The final result of the 1998 election was: ALP forty-four seats, National Party twenty-three, Liberal Party nine, One Nation eleven, Independents two. In the wash-up we lost the seats of Maryborough, Hervey Bay, Whitsunday, Ipswich West, Thuringowa and Mulgrave because of the One Nation vote. But we also won six from the Liberals, who had clearly been seen as having done a deal with the devil. We drew even for having the guts to take on Pauline Hanson and One Nation.

The One Nation phenomenon

Fighting Pauline Hanson nearly cost me the 1998 election. After I said in 1998 that I would not accept their preferences and I would not govern with them, we lost those six seats in the regions. Maybe it was swings and roundabouts because we won an extra six in the city, but I suspect that the price I paid for my stand was the ability for us to govern in our own right. We scraped in with a minority government but have been in power ever since.

Still, I would rather have lost than compromised. There are certain principles on which you should never compromise.

One Nation has now gone as a force. After getting 23 per cent of the vote in '98 and eleven seats in parliament, there is only one left in the current parliament at the time of writing, and they now count for practically nothing. Hanson came from Queensland, and Queensland got rid of her.

Some will see this as provocative but I believe that the Pauline Hanson One Nation phenomenon was really good for this country because it finally put to bed — put totally to bed or just to rest depending on whether you are an optimist or a pessimist — the remnants of the White Australia Policy and the intolerance that went with it. It's gone now. We've had the debate and it's finished; it's over and it's dead. Apart from the tiny percentage that will always have nonsensical views, the majority knows that Hansonism doesn't work and that One Nation doesn't work. The debate has enriched us. It damaged us in our region perhaps temporarily, but it has made us revalue multiculturalism. And that's really important for Australia.

Taking over the reins

I was sworn in at Government House and became premier on 26 June 1998; Jim Elder became the deputy premier. Jim and I had half the ministries each for the weekend before the full government was sworn in on Monday the 29th. Between us, we were the ministers for everything, so I can claim to have been in my time the Minister for Education, the Environment, the Minister for Primary Industries, Families, Health, Public

Works, Training, Industrial Relations, the Attorney-General, and the Minister for Justice as well — if only briefly!

Finally achieving government was a momentous occasion for a great many of us. But we had been down so many dry gullies we weren't going to let it go to our heads. We'd lost too often to become over-excited and we didn't know how long this would last. We had to face the fact that we had forty-four Labor members and the promise of a vote from Peter Wellington on certain conditions — while the Opposition also had forty-four votes.

Whether it is on the record or just one of those snappy, unrecorded exchanges, I remember Rob Borbidge calling out to me across the chamber words to the effect that he'd lasted two years and four months, and 'We'll see how long you last.' He added something like, 'You won't last four months.' Frankly, at that precise moment we were in no position to dispute him. At best we would make it through to a May 2001 election. Thanks to what became known as the Rorts Affair, we didn't get that far, instead going to the polls in February 2001. By then we had stayed in office for two years and eight months. The taunts of my predecessor as premier counted for nothing, except perhaps to make us more determined.

Way back on that day in late June of 1998, as always, since those early days with Nana, it was time to get cracking . . .

IN GOVERNMENT, 1998 AND BEYOND

Getting to work

It would be fair to say that my team and I threw ourselves wholeheartedly into the business of government. One of our early exercises was to hold a major trade and tourism summit involving more than 200 business leaders. We needed to find answers to the Asian economic turndown and the damage done to Queensland's reputation by international media reports on One Nation's anti-Asian policies. Various job-creation strategies were put forward. By the first half of 1999 we were fully in gear and delivered significant change in the form of new legislation in the areas of education, native title reform, prostitution, and industrial relations, among others. Boosting development and jobs growth were also very much on the agenda.

In the second half of 1998, my government established the Forde Inquiry to make sure we got to the heart of allegations of child abuse in Queensland's institutions. Part of that involved placing the youth detention system under scrutiny. By March of 1999 we were able to implement the strongest legislative protection from child abuse of any state in the Commonwealth with the passing of the new Child Protection Bill 1999. As Minister for Families, Youth and Community Care, Anna Bligh said at the time: 'After 30 years of inadequate and outdated legislation Queensland's child protection professionals have the best laws in the country to combat child abuse.' Among the many positive changes introduced, the legislation recognised the child's right to protection as paramount; introduced Australia's first Charter of Rights for Children in the Care of the State; enshrined the responsibilities of the state as guardian and regulated standards of care; reinforced the role of families in protecting children and the role of parents in making decisions about their children; and introduced criminal checks for prospective foster carers.[1]

We thought at the time this would be sufficient to protect Queensland children but as subsequent events showed, we still needed to do more work. Years of neglect were not going to be washed away easily.

Another area of concern was the protection of our remaining native forests in south-east Queensland. We had taken note of the environmental bad faith under Bjelke-Petersen; we learnt lessons. Our idea of good development is development delivered in cooperation with environmental principles and requirements, and built on the foundation of sustainability. We therefore entered into negotiations to secure agreement with all the relevant parties on the use of native forests on Crown land in that region. A reform of forestry practices, through the Regional Forest Agreement, ensured the protection of a huge amount of our forests and was secured with the agreement of the forestry industry as well as conservationists.

We had also had a long-standing issue with industrial laws in Queensland. To end the previous disharmony we brought back the concept of tripartite negotiation, a balanced process where all parties respect the independent umpire. That has led us to the happy position today where we have the least number of strikes of any state in Australia. In this tripartite approach, employer, government and union sit down together and work towards a fair outcome rather than more confrontation.

The Net Bet affair

We had not long been in government when we had cause to recall the old lesson that in politics you have to take the good with the bad, and the bad popped up in the form of the so-called Net Bet affair. Treasury had issued an internet gambling licence to a group named GOCORP. It turned out that MLA Bill D'Arcy, ministerial staff member Don Livingstone, and Ipswich Councillor Paul Pisascale — all people associated with the Labor Party — had an interest in the company. The Net Bet affair was an embarrassing time for us.

We dealt with the problem transparently by referring the matter to the Auditor-General for investigation. It was also referred to the CJC, the independent watchdog, to investigate what happened. Neither of the inquiries discovered any impropriety on the part of the government.

In terms of Net Bet, the Treasurer, David Hamill, argued strongly that due process had been followed in the issuing of the licence and the CJC found that was correct. But it was the public's perception of the decision that caused damage to the government.

We introduced retrospective legislation to ensure that no one in politics benefited out of Net Bet. The individuals concerned lost their right to have any private benefit from this internet casino; and GOCORP's licence would be revoked unless evidence was provided that the disqualified people had disposed of their interests without making a profit from the disposal. Further regulations prohibited people such as MPs and their families from taking interests in any companies holding interactive gambling rights in the future. The last thing I was going to tolerate was having my government tainted.

Electoral rorts

The government was not much more than two years old in August 2000. It was then that, after consultation with me and on behalf of the government, Attorney-General Matt Foley requested an inquiry by the Electoral Commissioner into allegations of electoral rorting within the Party in Queensland. At that point I knew that we — the government, myself personally, and the ALP in our state — were going to be in for some challenging times.[2] Why this development? It was precipitated by the claims of one Karen Ehrmann, a former Labor Party candidate who had recently been jailed for forging Party memberships in 1995 in order to stack pre-selection ballots for the Mundingburra by-election.

I had staked my claim to government in large part on the need for honesty and transparency so this was our first big test. Matt Foley rightly observed that, as the minister responsible for the Electoral Act, he was obliged 'to ensure public confidence in the integrity of the system'. To that I put my own rejoinder: 'Anyone who has broken the law should feel the full force of the law — justice not only has to be done, it has to be seen to be done'.[3] Here I was, eight years after the travel rorts affair, which resulted in me entering the political wilderness, wondering whether the same result was awaiting the government. I didn't know what would happen but I did know I had to do the right thing.

Once that initial inquiry was underway, events took a further turn when I referred matters to the CJC. It ordered a public inquiry into allegations of broader electoral rorting by the Labor Party, including an investigation of sitting Labor MPs. The inquiry was to be undertaken by a retired Supreme

Court Justice, Tom Shepherdson. I will readily confess that this was one of the low points of my life in politics. I was already feeling mortified over the electoral rorting that had been proved to have taken place in Townsville, now I was not only apprehensive but appalled at the possibility that there was more to come. This was my Party? I knew that when it came to preselections, factions played hard ball, but I didn't dream this extended to breaking the law. I had a difficult time disguising my emotions in response. Nevertheless, I was determined that the truth should be found and revealed, whatever the threat to political careers.

Incidents going back to the early '90s concerning false enrolment forms involving the AWU faction were revealed at the Shepherdson Inquiry, and the less than savoury role of some Party members began to surface. As soon as the evidence mounted about some of our Party officials' wrongdoing, I moved quickly to rid us of the trouble. After feelings of profound disappointment, I began instead to experience plain anger. Perhaps I might have been a bit more compassionate with the individuals involved, but I felt that their actions had let everyone down — the government, the Party, themselves and me. Being lenient or kind to them was not in order. Having fought so hard to win back government, it was difficult to accept that it could be lost because of this.

One day I was hit by a locomotive — John Budd, a prominent AWU party operative who'd gained preselection for the seat of Redlands, had allegedly used $30,000 of Bowman

Federal Executive's funds. This executive runs the campaign for the local federal candidate. What else could possibly go wrong? Joan and John Budd both went; anyone who had any taint had to go.

As for Grant Musgrove, the member for Springwood, I had difficult meetings with him and his brother. Terry Mackenroth and I met with them, and although Grant didn't want to go, there was no alternative.

Karen Ehrmann had already paid a heavy price. When this first broke I asked her about it and she told me there was no problem and she hadn't done anything wrong. Many people disappointed me in that way. People who had hidden things and, when confronted, never came forward with the full story. Although at an intellectual and moral level I know that demanding honesty was the right and correct path to take, and I took it, I still felt personally devastated at the extent of the activities that had been taking place. I said things would get worse, but this bad?

One of the bleakest outcomes of this mess was the loss of Jim Elder. Jim and I had been close friends for a long time. When Wayne Goss resigned in 1996 and I took over the leadership, few people in the Party honestly believed we could win. One of those believers was Jim Elder. He and I had worked closely together. On 22 November 2000, when I was in Osaka, Japan, Jim rang me to tell me that he was going to stand down. Jim had family members enrolled in his seat who lived outside his electorate — an untenable situation. For me, hearing the news was like being hit by a lightning bolt. Up until that point I had had no inkling that Jim had any involvement. The matter was so serious that I immediately cancelled the Korean leg of that trip to come home.

I experienced an acute sense of anger, betrayal — all those emotions. Jim had been my trusted deputy. You can't work closely with someone for almost five years without feeling strongly. Jim lost his whole career over some silly, family enrolments just to win ALP conference positions. It was plain dumb. And inexcusable. More than two years would pass before I could sit down and have a talk with Jim.

Jim has moved on; he's gone into business. I don't have any malice against him, and I do wish him well. But my biggest personal disappointment was that he didn't raise it with me up front.

Setting things right

Winning the 2001 election after such a public scandal was going to be a difficult proposition. Although it didn't seem possible, I was determined to give it my best shot as I knew the government had been travelling well up till then. I decided the best thing was to tell the truth, the whole truth and nothing but the truth, and to deal with everything head-on — firstly, to have it properly investigated, which is what has happened — and then to ensure that it never happened again, to clean up the Party and change the rules. In the final analysis, those who were betrayed most were the ordinary rank and file members of the Labor Party.

As the catalogue of misdeeds grew, I embarked on a full program of remediation. On 27 November I began by setting out publicly the first steps towards cleaning up the mess to make sure in future the Party conducted its business in a manner beyond reproach. With Elder gone I chose Terry Mackenroth as his replacement, whom I described as 'a strong son of a bitch who will stand next to me and kick and kick and kick those who have rorted the system'. He has proved to be precisely that and I consider his contribution to have been invaluable. I also declared my intention to clean out rorting in a more formal way.

I followed with an announcement on 30 November of an eight-point plan to eliminate rorters and rorting from the Party, along with the appointment of a new Executive Director for the Party, Tim Gartrell, whose job it would be to implement that plan. I had asked Tim to come up to Brisbane from Canberra, where he was a Party official. He was someone I knew, he'd done a good job in Canberra, and he was a good person. We needed the involvement of a national position or a national person to make sure that the right thing was done. It was important work and Tim did an excellent job — I don't think we could've done it without him. He has since become national ALP secretary.

With an election looming, it was time to move onto a more positive phase. As of December 2000, we were five candidates down as a result of resignations stemming from the electoral rorts affair. Having spelled out to all and sundry that I wanted honesty and integrity to be the watch words, I received a free hand from the ALP's Administrative Committee to choose a new team for the times ahead.

In January of 2001, I called the poll for 17 February, fully aware that we were facing an uphill battle, and that we would have to work to restore faith and trust in the ALP.

2001 election

The general political situation was already volatile before the revelations of August 2000. At the 1998 elections, a whopping 30 per cent of electors had not voted for the major parties at all, and Queensland was dotted with marginal seats: the ALP held twenty-seven of the eighty-nine electorates with margins of less than 5 per cent.[4]

We needed to be engaged on a lot of fronts: against the Liberals in south-east Queensland, against the Nationals in regional cities along the coast, and against One Nation or its rump wherever it might have sprung up, in rural or regional areas or even the outlying Brisbane suburbs. By now the Queensland Parliament comprised forty-five Labor, twenty-three Nationals, nine Liberals, six City–Country Alliance (CCA), six Independents. Ten of the CCA and Independents had been elected as One Nation members and we had won a forty-fifth seat in a by-election in 1999 after the resignation of a One Nation member.

But to top it off, new electoral boundaries meant my government would lose one seat anyway, with the ALP notionally holding forty-four seats and the Coalition thirty-three in a new parliament.

As an indication of how fragile things were for the Queensland ALP, Grant Musgrove won Springwood in 1995 by a very thin 0.5 per cent. Independents were also going to be crucial to our fortunes. And there was still the wildcard represented by One Nation, the Hansonites having won eleven seats and polled 22.68 per cent of the total Queensland vote in the 1998 election. Whatever else the Hansonites might do, I was acutely aware that their presence could still have the effect of confusing voters and throwing the final results into disarray. When she had not been able to persuade the West Australian Liberals to do preference deals in her favour, Pauline Hanson had got the hump and was now telling Queenslanders to put any sitting MPs last in their voting preferences.

The Administrative Committee gave me the power to select candidates, and I did so on the basis of ability; there was no conscious plan on my part to reduce any faction's influence in the choice of candidates. The deliberations proceeded through the middle of December and I clearly recall that some faction leaders were nervous about my decisions. Too bad; I was paying no heed to factional associations. I was keen to find more women candidates; it seemed about time that women were given a decent crack at state politics in Queensland.

That period was the first time in the history of the ALP, and probably the last, that a leader had had the power to select candidates. It was unheard of to have a direct control in choosing candidates. What a pity that it had come out of a crisis. I didn't miss the opportunity to put forward good candidates who I thought would hold the Party in good stead in the long term. On 20 December the Administrative Committee of the Party endorsed my choices. When the election came around, the result was an increased number of women in parliament, which gave us a more balanced caucus, among other benefits. And I am also proud to say that my candidate Michael Choi became Queensland's first Chinese–Australian member of parliament. We went on to win sixty-six of the eighty-nine seats.

2004 election

I would argue that 2004 was our toughest campaign and our finest result. Even though we won sixty-three seats compared to sixty-six in 2001, defending sixty-six seats was a heck of a tall order. And getting there was a rollercoaster journey; but then, election campaigns inevitably are. Mistakes aside, any aims and goals you might have as a politician are all dependent on one critical factor: winning an election and therefore the people's mandate.

On 13 January 2004, having first spoken to Governor Quentin Bryce, I announced that the election would be held on Saturday 7 February. By then we'd served a full term: two years, eleven months and twenty-one days, to be precise. What mostly prompted me was the report given on 9 January by Peter Forster, the reform specialist appointed by the government to implement the recommendations of the CMC's inquiry into child abuse and the effectiveness of the state Department of Families. I had earlier asked the CMC to examine certain cases of child abuse and systemic problems in the child protection area of the families department. The result was a public inquiry and a report recommending 110 improvements.

Mr Forster, who had led the police and government reforms following the Fitzgerald Inquiry of 1987–89, stated that he would produce a blueprint for reform and for the establishment of a new Department of Child Safety which he would submit to a new Cabinet following the state election. The changes he was about to bring about were urgently needed. Despite my government making massive improvements to the funding, staffing and legislation dealing with child protection, some deep-seated problems remained. The system had let down a number of children who were subjected to continuing abuse, and this had been exposed in the media. Strong action was called for. I pledged to implement the reforms.

On 12 January I was able to tell Queenslanders that the next Queensland government would be in such good financial shape that it would be able to fully fund all the recommendations. Whether or not the next government would be led by me, no one could know.

We went into the campaign with another major black mark against us in the minds of the public, and this was in the area of health. Despite our practice of publishing waiting time figures on our Internet site four times a year, figures which demonstrated a massive reduction in waiting times under the ALP, the Opposition had sufficiently talked up health as an issue. Journalists were routinely using phrases such as 'the health crisis' and 'growing waiting times'. According to our pollsters, so deeply entrenched was this negative perception in the minds of the voting public that no information we produced to the contrary would change it. In other words, although according to the health department our waiting times were the best on record, we were in an unwinnable position on this one.

To further complicate our prospects of being re-elected, on the afternoon of 14 January I was told that Tourism Minister Merri Rose had been referred to in a report by the government's Workers' Compensation Regulatory Authority in connection with bullying allegations. It was regarding a claim for workers' compensation by one of her former staff members. I called her into my office where she strongly and strenuously denied the allegations, but she realised that she could not remain as a minister with this hanging over her head in an election campaign and so she did the appropriate thing by the government and resigned.

Merri also referred allegations in the report to the CMC, in a letter drafted after her resignation.

At 6.30 that night — the end of the second day of campaigning — I called a media conference to announce her resignation. I told the conference I had also written to the CMC and had made specific reference to the point that Merri Rose strongly and strenuously denied the allegations.

Meanwhile, I had to concentrate on electioneering. Election campaigns are non-stop. In Queensland, they mean twenty-six days of constant interaction with the public, the media, fellow Cabinet ministers, members of parliament who feel neglected, members of parliament who feel they should be contributing more, members of parliament who feel they have a contribution to make, the campaign team, the Party organisation, and hundreds of others. So the demands start early in the morning and go on until very late at night. If the marathon is a race of twenty-six miles, then I suppose it's entirely fitting that the minimum election campaign is fixed at twenty-six days. The effect on the body may well be about the same.

The Party leaders are followed on this marathon by a pack of journalists. Their needs and my needs, however, are not the same. Reporters like to finish each day in a comfortable hotel — and why wouldn't they? — while I need to influence as many people as possible in a limited number of days. So I have to visit as many electorates as I can.

To make one of our key announcements, we travelled by road into the beautiful Sunshine Coast hinterland to a spot of woodland at Elanda ranger station in Cooloola National Park. Our news was that, if re-elected, we would end broad-scale tree clearing of remnant vegetation — with or without federal government support. Within three years the clearing 'dozers in remnant vegetation areas would be mothballed, I said.[5] In real terms, that meant moving from a situation where an average of 250,000 hectares of remnant vegetation is cleared each year to practically zero remnant clearing. Sadly, that positive momentum was diluted by the next crisis in the campaign, one which was all of my own making. Even a seasoned campaigner such as myself is still capable of the odd gaffe, as I was soon to discover.

At election time, the normally uninterested all-music FM stations suddenly want five minutes with political leaders. But theirs is a different kind of radio to my weekly Friday spot on 4BC and B105. In 2004 I found myself answering such questions as, 'Do you prefer hot or cold?' and 'Are you a jockey shorts or Y-fronts man?', hardly questions to which any answer of mine might change a person's vote — at least I hope not! But it was while I was at one of these stations in Cairns that I made a silly comment that resulted in major headlines. The repartee between the breakfast team and myself was flying fast and furious and, in a light-hearted manner off-air, I turned to Heather and said, in a voice which no one further than a metre away could hear, that I would need a lobotomy to pose as Opposition Leader Lawrence Springborg in a mock debate that was being proposed by one of the radio station's 'on air' crew.

I confess I should not have made such a remark. On the other hand, the remark was not broadcast, it was not made to a reporter, it was not directed at anyone other than my wife, and no one else heard it — apart from a reporter from *The Australian*. The reporter said nothing to me at the time, nor later in the morning when I held a media conference, nor even later in the day when she joined me at a shopping centre where I spent half an hour or so chatting to local people.

Of course I didn't mean it. Of course it was not meant to be an insult. Of course there was no malice in it. But the reporter was determined to beat it up into a major story. Later I discovered that she had approached people in the studio and that they'd told her that they hadn't heard me say anything. In the end she wrote a piece that alleged I had made an awful and serious remark at a radio station, suggesting also that it would have major repercussions. I was amazed to read the story the next morning in *The Australian* — a newspaper otherwise regarded as a serious paper of record — presented as a beat-up of Fleet Street proportions. Immediately I rang Lawrence to explain the circumstances of the remark and to apologise for it. I have to say that the Leader of the Opposition accepted my apology and did not seek to exploit it. But the rest of the media then focused on the comment instead of our major announcements.

My next highly publicised run-in with a political figure was with Bob Katter, the Independent federal member for Kennedy. During the election campaign I underlined my determination to keep Queensland as the engine room of Australia and at the same time spelt out a program of reform for the state over the next few years. On the reform agenda were a range of difficult issues, including the sugar industry. Bob organised a number of protests to try to get us to back down and change our views, but I refused to do so. Without reform the Queensland sugar industry, and indeed the sugar industry generally, will not survive. Unfortunately, when a riled up Bob and his supporters ambushed me in Cairns as I was leaving a news conference, things got a little out of hand.

I had no problem with Bob Katter bringing the farmers to try to embarrass me. It did concern me though that there was a young child among the protesters who could well have been hurt. I consider protest to be important, but the idea of physically endangering children in the process appals me. There were people milling around our car; the car was blocked at the traffic lights; and even though the lights had turned green, we could not move forward. When the cars started to bank up, the situation was patently unsafe. I would have thought the protesters should have known better. But that's politics.

We moved down to Mackay and the sugar protests continued. I emerged from the ABC studios to find a sizeable, unhappy crowd had gathered. We managed to have a civil and sensible conversation, heated though it was at a couple of points. And then things took a turn for the bizarre. While I was speaking to the protesters, someone came up and tapped me on the back of the shoulder. To my surprise, I spun round to find myself face-to-face with the former National Party candidate for Whitsunday who had been disendorsed for past association with the Nazi Party.

Next stop was Mackay Hospital, where I was launching a strategy to deal with strokes. We were gathered around a bed looking at the equipment while I made my speech. Part-way through, a woman came forward and asked what I was going to do about the 'beast men'. I frankly did not have a clue what she was talking about. She turned out to be part of an organisation that wanted to undermine George Bush, Dick Cheney and a string of other people in the US administration.

We left Mackay shortly after, but my 'interesting' day was not yet over. At Yeppoon, we went to the shopping centre and I was told that a person who was keen to catch up with me was roaming about trying to attract the attention of the media. Apparently it was the popular National Party member, Vince Lester, who was actually retiring from politics, but he never did manage to corner me.

Then it was on to Bundaberg. There a National Party candidate by the name of Messenger — he subsequently won the seat — jumped out and bailed me up in front of the local TV reporter about something to do with fishing. He ended his complaints by saying, 'Don't you shoot the messenger.' Seemingly, it was the only line he could come up with for the cameras. As I boarded the plane heading back to Brisbane, I wondered, given all the odd political behaviour I'd encountered, whether the full moon had come early. Life on the campaign trail in Queensland had become strange indeed.

On 22 January I launched one of the most far-reaching plans of the campaign: the $110 million strategy to further slash public hospital waiting times for operations. We had already succeeded in making our public hospitals the best in the country — as the Productivity Commission had previously established — and, by extension, some of the best in the world. The plan targeted problem areas where people were still waiting too long for operations. This worked effectively because soon after the election we were able to start treating extra patients.

Later that evening the Nationals' leader, Lawrence Springborg, and I co-hosted a major gathering on the august Speaker's Green of Parliament House to celebrate the Chinese New Year. In attendance were Australian–Chinese and those with some Chinese ancestry as well as those from other ethnic backgrounds. It proved to be a remarkable and memorable evening.

This demonstration of cross-party support for multiculturalism during the election campaign was an important step for the Nationals to take and I congratulate them for doing so. Not so long ago the National Party was anti-academic, anti-women in the workplace and anti just about anyone who wasn't born in Queensland, especially if they didn't believe in their god. To have Lawrence Springborg, in the middle of an election campaign, talking positively about multiculturalism was an indication that the re-education of a rump of Queenslanders away from judging people on the basis of their colour, name or beliefs and towards more open and tolerant values — a process we had begun years before — was truly beginning to work. Clearly, such values were now becoming acceptable across the political board.

Another highlight of the campaign was my stay at Barcaldine, in the heart of Queensland. This was National Party territory but also the birthplace of the Australian Labor Party, which grew from the shearers' fight for a fair go at the end of the nineteenth century. I popped into Pat Ogden's pub to have a chat with some of the locals, listen to their views on life and buy a few beers. Pat is a Labor legend out in Barcy and he played a major role in the establishment of the Workers' Heritage Centre in the town. Next day, I was joined by some of the media for my usual 5.30 a.m. walk. It was a glorious dawn with only birdsong to break the silence of the outback.

Returning to the centre of Barcaldine, we bumped into some lovely ladies who were sitting outside the town's old cinema, waiting to go inside to clean up. We popped our heads in to find that this huge old shed of a building looks today much as it would have done in the 1920s when it was first built — except for the wear and tear — even down to the double canvas chairs. Later that morning I launched a policy at the Workers' Heritage Centre to help local councils renovate their memorials.

Among the problems with calling the election in January was the summer heat: there were days when it reached 40 degrees, with high humidity to make it even worse. One of these unforgettable days was in Townsville when we launched our far-reaching policy to make a full year of prep school available to all Queensland children. We had chosen Rasmussen State School for the launch because it was taking part in the prep-year trial and so we could show the assembled media how things were progressing and what sort of accommodation would be needed in every school. One of our 'advance' people had visited the school and made sure everyone was happy with the arrangements; she had decided that an outdoor courtyard under a shade screen would be suitable for the media conference. Well, the area had been cool enough when she visited. But on the day we stood there, it was like the inside of a Turkish bath. Sweat poured off everyone; it was difficult to breathe let alone think. To top it all off, although we were all as red as beetroots, thanks to the colour of the shadecloth we appeared purple on screen — not a good look.

A further important initiative was our announcement of an office of urban management and infrastructure coordination tasked with managing and supporting the dramatic growth we are experiencing in south-east Queensland, Australia's fastest growing region. I named my deputy, Terry Mackenroth, as the person who would be at the helm; I felt he was well able to manage this responsibility in addition to his role as treasurer. In identifying needs in areas such as water supply, sewage, energy, schools, roads, railways and open space — some of the essential things that make the south-east so attractive and liveable — the direct link between the budget process regarding infrastructure requirements and the urban management office itself would be invaluable. As I said at the time, 'We will not let our popularity become a curse'.[6]

* * *

When election day rolled around, I was immensely proud of my family. As parents, Heather and I took pleasure in seeing our children through another rite of passage — this was the first time Larissa, Denis and Matthew had voted, which made it the first time we all voted together. I was deeply touched that my children wanted to do that with me. Even before the results came through, before I realised that we had won again — with the second biggest majority the Labor Party has ever had in Queensland — (sixty-three seats) — 7 February 2004 was a particularly special day.

That night the five of us travelled in two cars out to the Boondall tally room, talking to each other by phone. It was a thrill for me that they were excited by the occasion. It was just wonderful to be there with my family and to have them present for the re-election. I cherish the family photographs taken of that occasion.

Positive politics won for the ALP in Queensland in 2004 because our focus was on highlighting what we would do for education, health and the environment, all the things that were important in our long-term vision for the state's future. In contrast, the National Party chose to mount negative attacks on me at every opportunity. Perhaps they were trying to take some shine off me so that they might have a chance of winning in 2007. Whatever the motive, Queenslanders are too astute about politics to fall for that kind of strategy. Sometimes

Mum and Dad, Edna and Arthur Beattie, just after World War II.

The Beattie children at 'Roma', Condobolin. This is the only existing photograph with all seven kids present. My brother David died in 1956 at the age of eight. Back row (left to right): Lynette, Edna and Joan. Middle row (left to right): Bill, Arthur and David (with flag). In front: me.

A very young me!

Mum posing in August 1957 in front of the school bus. She helped to establish the bus service that picked up kids from the bush and got them to school in Condobolin. She died six weeks after the photograph was taken. I keep this picture on my desk at home to remind me where I come from.

Grade 1D at Condobolin primary school, 1959. I'm in the middle of the second row from the front.

Annie Jane Esbensen, Nana, who gave me my start in life.

Country towns are great to grow up in. I count myself lucky to have spent my childhood in such a great environment as Atherton.

I love sport, and at school I took part in as many activities as I could. Here I am with my hockey team in Ipswich, 1965 (back row, third from left).

Atherton, March 1968. The Scouts was another way for me to experience a great outdoor life.

I was the only one in my family who had the chance to go to university. Luckily I won a Commonwealth scholarship which made it possible for me to study Arts/Law at the University of Queensland. If only I had such abundant hair today!

UNIVERSITY OF QUEENSLAND	
Name	PETER D. BEATTIE
Student No.	040202-712
Month & Year of Birth	11-1952
Course	B.A./LL.B.
Attendance	FULL-TIME
Subjects	LA1CR LA2CL LA2LH HY202 GT201
Film No.	13 060

1972

BEATTIE

SIGNATURE

Submit your student card to Enrolments Section should any changes be necessary

ABOVE A real 'mug' shot.

LEFT My graduation day, when I received my family's first ever degree.

BELOW Heather and me at St John's College — true love.

ABOVE Taking part in an Amnesty International demonstration in Brisbane, August 1980. Also in the photo is Father Jim Soorley (far left) who would later become Lord Mayor of Brisbane.

LEFT Dr Denis Murphy and I setting off to conquer Western Queensland by light aircraft, in October 1982. Denis was a great leader whom I truly admired … but a terrible pilot!

ABOVE At the Berlin Wall in 1987. The Wall was a manifestation of political bloody mindedness of the worst order.

LEFT The end of an era. Sir Joh Bjelke-Petersen (at left) leaving the Fitzgerald Inquiry in December 1988. I was a Labor Party solicitor during part of the inquiry which proved to be the start of a new, cleaner Queensland.

The marriage of politics and family — how Heather coped with three children under two years *and* politics is beyond me.

LEFT Labour Day March, May 1987. Me, Heather, Matthew (in the top of the pram) Larissa and Denis. BELOW At the rally for Democracy, August 1989, with Heather and the kids.

My son Matthew helping me to lodge my nomination for party pre-selection for the state seat of Brisbane Central, May 1988.

BELOW Party leader Wayne Goss giving a speech at the launch of my campaign for the Brisbane seat. I could always rely on Wayne's support.

At last to Government. Being sworn in as Queensland Premier at Government House in Brisbane, June 1998. Jim Elder (at right) was sworn in as Deputy Premier in the same ceremony.

After 200 years of failed Indigenous policy, we need a fresh approach. Here Noel Pearson and I discuss plans for Aboriginal welfare reform by the banks of the Bloomfield River at Wujal Wujal, 1999.

Labor leaders working with the Liberal Prime Minister at the 2004 COAG meeting in Canberra. Left to right: South Australia Premier Mike Rann, me, New South Wales Premier Bob Carr, Victorian Premier Steve Bracks and Northern Territory Chief Minister Claire Martin.

The lighter side of politics — AFL football unites the premiers.
Left to right: Bob Carr in Sydney Swans' colours; Mike Rann in a Port Adelaide jersey and Adelaide Crows scarf; me in the mighty Brisbane Lions' gear; Western Australia Premier Geoff Gallop in a West Coast Eagles jersey and Fremantle Dockers scarf; and Steve Bracks in an Essendon jersey and Collingwood scarf.

LEFT At the Commonwealth Heads of Government Meeting in Queensland, 2002, with Thabo Mbeki, President of the Republic of South Africa. My fight against apartheid in South Africa helped fire my interest in politics.

RIGHT Signing an agreement with Sir Michael Somare, Prime Minister of Papua New Guinea, in 2002. Prime Minister Somare is an old friend of Queensland.

LEFT With Helen Clark, Prime Minister of New Zealand, in Brisbane, 2003. Queensland and New Zealand are great mates, continuing the ANZAC tradition.

RIGHT Queen Elizabeth II won the hearts of Queenslanders when she visited in 2002.

LEFT Jiang Zemin, President of the People's Republic of China, visited North Queensland in 1999, and we enjoyed a day of swimming and snorkelling.

BELOW (left to right): Wang Yeping (the President's wife), Tom Burns (Chair of the Queensland–China Council), Jiang Zemin, me and Heather.

LEFT Founder of the Goodwill Games, Ted Turner, his wife, Jane Fonda, Heather and me at a dinner in 1999.

RIGHT Singing 'Waltzing Matilda' at Parliament House with Lee Kernaghan, Ted Turner and Slim Dusty during the 2001 Goodwill Games.

In 2003 the Queensland Government announced its decision to ban tree clearing in the state — a smart move.

AAP IMAGE/TONY PHILLIPS

Greeting 'John Howard' during the Queensland Labour Day Rally through the streets of Brisbane in 2004.

Talking with Prime Minister John Howard, US President George Bush and Victorian Premier Steve Bracks, in Canberra, 2003. Despite disagreeing with many of the Howard Government's policies, I have worked hard at having a good working relationship with the Prime Minister, which has yielded benefits for Queensland.

In 2003 I toured the new Suncorp Stadium, showing former premier Sir Joh Bjelke-Petersen and his wife Lady (Flo) Bjelke-Petersen a modern Queensland.

Running with our dog Rusty in the 2004 election campaign. I am the one with my feet on the ground!

BELOW February, 2004. A family that votes together stays together — I hoped I could still count on the children! Left to right: Denis, me, Matthew, Larissa and Heather.

NEWSPIX/NEWS LTD

NEWSPIX/ROB MACCOLL

politicians underestimate the public. It's true that I didn't particularly like the National Party ads on a personal level, but they were totally ineffective and did us no harm whatsoever politically. While the other side was wasting its energy on those ads, they missed a chance to ram home some positive policies for themselves.

While we were ecstatic with the 2004 election result, it provided a long-term dark cloud on the horizon. The cloud is bad news for the National Party, good news for the Liberal Party. That is because when the political pendulum goes against Labor next, the Liberal Party will be the big winners and for the first time in Queensland's history, the Liberals will be the dominant conservative party in Queensland at state level.

The practical art

Among the tools for making a difference in society are those of democratic politics — they are the means by which, in our system, political parties might gain government. And the only good reason, in my assessment, for any individual or group to seek government is the desire to make a difference. Obviously, in order to do that, you have to learn to play the political game. To be honest, I was good at that and I enjoyed it, but I never lost sight of the big picture. What I didn't do was take shortcuts and line up with the old political machine; had I done so, change and reform would not have been possible.

Politics is often described as the art of the possible, and experience tells us that is certainly true. The hard work of developing realistic visionary policies which, if and when implemented, will bring about positive rather than negative outcomes for real human beings, is a practical and not particularly glamorous business, and one where governments and political parties do not always achieve what they set out to do.

State governments have control over many actions that result in life-altering experiences for thousands of people. The decisions — or lack of them — of a government can irrevocably change the course of someone's life. The role of government as a positive force in people's lives is, in the developed societies, not much more than 150 years old. So we're still getting the hang of it, really. New eras bring with them new challenges and to be involved in the 'practical art' means you have to keep tackling them afresh.

In my own case, and after about seven years in power in Queensland, people have a right to ask: Well, what difference have you made? What have you done to change Queensland? Are people better off now than they were in June 1998 when you were handed the keys to the machinery of government? My short answer to that question is 'Yes'. I believe we have made a positive difference in every area of government. I am confident that any fair reading of our achievements — we have issued a summary of these each year — will show this to be true. But I won't subject readers here to the dozens of pages that a listing of these would involve. Our most significant achievement was jobs, jobs and jobs, and reducing our trend unemployment to 5 per cent by November 2004 and then below that soon afterwards.

Achievements

In late 2004 I was asked to list my top ten achievements since entering parliament. It took a lot of pain to boil down scores of worthy initiatives but in the end I nominated this list, which still holds as I write today in 2005:

- Reforming education and reducing class sizes, adding an extra year of pre-school, achieving a higher retention rate, and increasing school-based apprenticeships to enable children to have a better chance of reaching their full potential.
- Turning Queensland from a narrow-based economy into the Smart State, with a focus on using new technologies and innovation to create thousands of long-term, new age, value-adding jobs in traditional and new industries. Developing new industries in aviation and biotechnology, and expanding export education.
- Providing the systems and budgets to enable doctors, nurses and health workers to cut waiting times for public hospital operations to the best on record, in a health system which has been judged the most effective in Australia.

- Creating more jobs in Queensland than in any other state to deliver the lowest unemployment rates since 1978. Creating 44 per cent of all jobs in Australia over the last year and reducing unemployment to our target of 5 per cent.
- Cutting crime rates such as armed robbery, unarmed robbery, breaking and entering, and car theft to the lowest in ten years so that Queenslanders can feel safer in their homes.
- Placing a halt on new tree clearing on leasehold and freehold properties throughout Queensland after allocating a package of $150 million to preserve South-East Queensland's precious native forests in a go-it alone decision despite fierce opposition from the National Party.
- Being responsible for major reforms, both as chairman of the Parliamentary Criminal Justice Committee and as premier, that enable all Queenslanders to live in an open, honest society with equal rights and without fear of discrimination, in a multicultural and tolerant society.
- After decades of governments throwing up their hands in surrender, giving Indigenous communities on Cape York the opportunity to kick out grog, reclaim their lives and give their children a future.

- More than doubling the child protection budget, doubling the number of frontline child protection workers, and boosting funding to people with disabilities by more than 40 per cent.
- Ensuring that after seven years in office we maintain the healthiest economy in the country, with a rate of growth well above the rest of Australia.

Part III

VISIONS AND VALUES

I t used to be said that you learned good behaviour at your parents' knee — true in my case, if you substitute Nana for Mum and Dad. Maybe there was also another kind uncle or aunt that took an interest in your welfare and who you were happy to look up to. There might have been another role model or two among your teachers — true again for me. The Church rounded off the process by providing the basic moral precepts: thou shalt not kill, not steal, and so forth. These means by which society guided the moral and ethical development of the young may have been basic, but they were effective. They seemed to have worked for me, inasmuch as I did not go off the rails or cause the community any particular grief — though my political opponents in recent years may have a different view about that.

But the world is becoming more complicated. Kids have to deal with numerous influences; they are subjected to relentless marketing, most of which reinforces the idea that you have to have lots of 'stuff' in order to be happy. I would argue that only by promoting positives that go beyond selfish individualism can we hope to have a happy younger generation, one that is not alienated but grows up to make its own constructive contribution.

To try to have a vision for yourself and those around you, informed by good and generous values instead of meanness and selfishness, has always been an ambition of mine, as it has been for many other people. Not that these things come naturally: developing good values is like training any other aspect of yourself. In a world where there are so many negative forces at work, it's tempting to say, 'Why should I bother?' But cynicism is too easy and comfortable.

What do people need in order to develop a positive vision for their future and the future of those around them? Here's my basic list: equal opportunity in education and employment; access to good health care; moral and material justice in a tolerant multicultural society, rather than privilege and discrimination; good political leadership and constructive party politics; an efficient, representative political system that takes notice of tomorrow, especially our children's tomorrow; and an open society that promotes and works towards these things, one in which people feel wanted and are allowed to contribute their best. To me, that is the ultimate vision.

LEARNING FROM OTHERS

A range of influences

No one in politics comes fully formed and dropped from the sky — at least not in my experience! In my own development I owe a debt to a number of mentors, role models and inspirations. Among these are politicians, identities, people I've learned from through my adult years. Not all of them I've known personally. It has been salutary to study the work and the behaviour of leaders of previous governments, and also to look beyond Australia's shores at what has happened overseas.

Australian political leaders

At federal level, Gough Whitlam and Bob Hawke were my two major influences and, to a lesser extent, Paul Keating. I won't hide from the fact that many of my early education ideas for the betterment of Queensland I derived from Gough Whitlam. In the aftermath of the Dismissal the assessment of Gough's government wasn't entirely fair. Though he subsequently wrote to try to redress the record and restore some balance, the general perception of him and his government still isn't what it should be. But politics is never fair, and anyone who sits around waiting for it to be fair will die a disgruntled and unhappy old man or woman. You have to try to make the best of what is often an unfair environment.

Having a vision for your society is the primary inspiration of Gough Whitlam. And, as a corollary, the importance of having the drive to take you where you would like to go. One of my predecessors as premier once said that state governments were about management and there was no room for a vision, or words to that effect. I have always considered that wrong. Government at all levels requires a vision and a plan — something you are never going to have, by the way, with a government comprising only independents. But then again, not all governments can manage to develop and project a coherent vision and plan. If you don't have a bigger picture in mind for your society, and a strategy for implementing that picture, if you're only going to manage the day-to-day business, then you might as well get a large accountancy firm in to do it. A real vision for what you want to achieve is fundamental. In my view politicians are here to make people's lives better, and it's an honour to be in the job.

Gough's overall vision was what made him so policy

focused. People might argue with the expression of that vision but there is no question he had one. When the Whitlam government was dismissed, I was devastated that that could happen in our democracy. The will of the people was basically overturned by a backroom deal. People can say what they like about the detail but that's what happened. Yes, he and his government were eventually voted out for all sorts of reasons — politically the government was not doing well and there were other factors influencing why he lost. But that way of bringing about the end of a government was not good for democracy.

Following such a coup, Malcolm Fraser was never going to be given — in the eyes of many people — credibility for his prime ministership. I don't think his prime ministership has been well regarded and I don't think it ever will be. He was seen to have obtained the top job in a stigmatised way and the stigma didn't go away. Plus, if your measure is social progress through good policies, the Fraser government was forgettable. Politically, Malcolm Fraser will be remembered for the Dismissal, and possibly for having appointed John Howard as his Treasurer.

Malcolm Fraser has nevertheless worked hard in retirement and gained respect from many quarters. Even if he'll never be regarded as one of our great prime ministers, I would happily applaud his views on South Africa and his position on a number of other international matters and the good works he has engaged in generally. Deep down, there's probably a better person in Malcolm Fraser than people saw in 1975. And I think if people try to make amends or ask for forgiveness or try to better themselves they should be given credit for doing that. I try to be fair-minded about the achievements of politicians from all sides as, clearly, not all the good batsmen or bowlers are in the one team — there are good people on both sides of politics.

After Whitlam's influence, I would value most highly that of Bob Hawke, a man with whom I get on well personally, too. Prior to winning government, he and Bill Hayden put in the work to develop worthwhile policies; they rebuilt the credibility of Labor for government.

As he didn't ultimately land the top job, Bill Hayden may never get some of the credit he's entitled to, but he was responsible for the Reconstruction and Recovery elements in the Party's platform leading into 1983, to which Bob Hawke added the third plank of Reconciliation. It was an unbeatable combination in the end. Hayden worked hard to get the re-engineering happening, but Hawke delivered government.

Another breakthrough of the Hawke period was that discipline came back into the Labor Party within both the caucus and the Cabinet. Gough had not been well served by some of his ministers and at first the need to be tough and firm about those things wasn't high on his agenda. By contrast, Hawke proved to be effective at instituting discipline.

It was Bob Hawke who showed that you can bring people together and get out among the public with a positive idea.

That worked for Australia's benefit and I think we're a better place for it. (Economic reform is a key example: the Hawke–Keating reforms paved the way for Australia's current strong economic position.) We've been able to put this into practice in Queensland, and as a result we have delivered on the 5 per cent unemployment target. We can do it better at a state level because we're smaller, we can easily get out and talk in the communities. You won't always get consensus and you always get a small percentage of interest groups who want to be disruptive if they don't get their way. But most Australians do want to work together and they expect you to work with other political parties. Hawke's consensus model probably became a little tired by the end of his government. But it worked for most of the time. Policies that have usefully endured from the Hawke–Keating days include the floating of the dollar, deregulation of the banks, and changes to education funding; these have led to an open and competitive economy.

Paul Keating had an influence on my thinking, particularly on Indigenous issues and our need to focus on Asian trade. His approach was crash through or crash, and in that regard he resembles Gough. Paul had very firm and not always encompassing views. My preference is to take a consensus approach. As I've already stated, politics is the art of achieving what's possible, and to that end I think that consensus produces better results. That doesn't mean you have to be weak or unclear; I'm clear about my views. But one person's views can always be improved by a consensus model of Cabinet.

Often a minister will come up with something sharper, so you pick up that idea. No one can be right all of the time. If you're right only 60 per cent of the time, you're on Einstein's level.

Among state politicians, Neville Wran and Don Dunstan both rank highly with me. Neville Wran was impressive as President of the National Executive. He ran a tough meeting; he was totally no-nonsense. And he was a hero. Where Gough lost, Wran won. He was an inspiring leader. Over his ten years as Premier of New South Wales, he made things happen. For instance, he worked on public transport questions; he rehabilitated Darling Harbour. His approach was 'do something, leave something, make something', which I find appealing.

Don Dunstan, on the other hand, was someone who made his mark in terms of cultural and social policies. He had a certain influence on me as I was developing my ideas. From him I concluded that a creative and innovative society is ultimately more productive and fulfilling for its people — his legacy lives on.

This is going to sound sacrilegious, but just as I embraced the reform process from Wayne Goss, I also learned from Mike Ahern, National Party Premier; they were both very good. It is my belief that you can take something useful from governments of the other persuasion. I got on well with Bill Gunn, the Deputy Premier of the National Party, and I admired Ahern's dignity when he went down with the flag flying, knocked over by his own party. The biography published about him, and which I launched, reflects a man who was committed to doing the right thing.[1] He has had the respect of history for it. I learnt from Ahern the importance of honesty under difficult circumstances. That was a lesson I have had to call into play, especially when I struck problems with people within Labor ranks.

World figures

Bill Clinton is high on my list of world leaders whom I think we would do well to heed. Having met him on a couple of occasions and also having twice listened to him making an address, he is without a doubt one of the best speakers I've ever heard in my life. I understand his personal shortcomings and failings — the question of his infidelity, for example — and how people are inclined to judgment on the basis of that. Be that as it may, in March 2000 when I was in Columbia, the capital of South Carolina, I had the privilege to hear him make a speech about world events which can only be described as truly memorable.

That evening I was present at the invitation of the then governor of the state, Jim Hodges, a Democrat who later unfortunately fell to the Republicans as a result of the Bush push. South Carolina and Queensland have a sister-state relationship, and on the strength of that I was visiting on a trade mission. Jim Hodges organised for me to meet Bill Clinton in a small group before the dinner. We shook hands and he talked about his visit to the Daintree and Port Douglas in Queensland as if it had been yesterday instead of four years previously.

Clinton was still President at the time and in his speech he talked about the Middle East and the world in general. He stressed how people have got to get over the hatred, let it go, in order to move on; again and again, he emphasised the importance of being positive.

It's a philosophy that I share. To say that Clinton's speech moved me is an understatement. It galvanised me into focusing on the positive possibilities for all of us.

On 12 September 2001, I made a ministerial statement in parliament, proposing that we should adjourn for a day as a mark of respect for those who died in the terror attacks in the US, stating:

> If this must be a day that changed the world, then we must ensure that it ultimately changes the world for the better. Each of us must be committed to that purpose. The perpetrators of this outrage must be dealt with. We cannot let terrorism succeed. They cannot be allowed to go unpunished. But then we must all work to create a world where we defuse the hate that fuels terrorism . . .[2]

In 2002, by which time he was no longer President, Clinton made a speech at Georgetown University. This time his subject was education, always one of my passions. In the Georgetown speech he made a link between the fundamental role of education in lifting people's standard of living and the ending of terrorism. Those who are denied education have to be given a chance. We have to provide opportunities.

Clinton's broader messages must be kept alive: if your aim is to end up with a better world and you're really going to build something enduring, you can't let anger prevail. The need to resolve conflict and strive for world peace is fundamental. Even if our own issues and concerns are on a less dramatic scale than we might find in Afghanistan or Iraq, these values are still relevant to our lives in our state and this country and we should proclaim them at every opportunity. Without a doubt, those two Clinton speeches inspired me and also further confirmed views I had been forming over a long time.

You hear anecdotes about Clinton's charm and charisma, and one personal interaction with him did much to endear him to me. After he had retired, I was sitting next to him at a Brisbane dinner to raise money for charity; Heather was seated on my left. While we were all chatting informally, Heather's mobile rang. It was our son, Matthew, phoning from home. I asked Bill Clinton if he would say hello, and he was happy to oblige. So Matthew found himself chatting for several minutes with the very personable former leader of the world's biggest superpower.

Nelson Mandela is another inspiring leader. He is a man who had the guts to resist. And when he came back into the political sphere after his incarceration ended, he had no special hatred for his gaolers but instead carried a clear vision for rebuilding his society. Sadly, I have never had the chance to meet Mandela but the new South African President, Thabo Mbeki, was here for CHOGM when I met him, and he, too, is most impressive.

Another world leader who I found to be interesting in person — not that I can relate to his politics — was Jiang Zemin, an extremely well-read and forceful individual. Heather and I hosted the now former President of China for almost a day on the Great Barrier Reef off Cairns and Port Douglas. He made great conversation and with good English. We discussed biotechnology and medical research and we also touched on what was happening in China. You would expect the President of China to be perceptive, which he most decidedly was. It was fascinating to talk about change and about managing change in a developing society. The setting up of economic development zones was something he'd done very well. I found him to be one of the most interesting people I have spoken to on these subjects.

Also present that day was Tom Burns, who has a special connection with China. In 1971, as National President of the ALP, Tom played a leading role in Prime Minister Gough Whitlam's historic delegation to China when Australia officially recognised the People's Republic of China. He later became deputy premier in the Goss government. One of the very few Australian political leaders to have met three generations of Chinese leaders, Tom has been deeply involved in economic and cultural contacts with China ever since.

In one of the lighter moments of Jiang's visit, Heather, Tom and I went swimming with Jiang off a Great Barrier Reef island. Accompanying us were about a dozen of the visiting dignitary's bodyguards who formed a circle around us, presumably to protect their leader from any shark attack — evidently, if any sharks had appeared, one of these men would have been obliged to sacrifice himself. As we emerged from the water, somebody made a remark about two beached whales. I wasn't going to tell Jiang what that referred to. Among the private photos taken that day, one or two tell a story. Standing around dripping wet, Tom and I looked like your classic 'beached whales'.

A little later, as we neared Port Douglas, I went to thank the specialist Queensland police squad who had provided protection all day. The Special Emergency Response Team was stationed in a secluded area on the upper deck. As I entered the smallish space, I was taken aback at the sight of all these extremely tall and well-armed individuals. Unbeknown to me, the President had followed me in, and he didn't seem the slightest bit fazed. Unlike me, he was used to this level of security.

I met George W. Bush while he was Governor of Texas, at a time when he was considering running for president. We talked for half an hour or so about Texas, the USA,

Queensland, Australia and relations in general. He mentioned he was being pushed to run for the presidency and talked about the money that had been raised. He also spoke of his friendship with John Newcombe, the tennis player, about rugby union, Australian beer, IT, biotechnology, and the BIO Annual International Convention being held that year. I found him to be friendly and relaxed. The enduring recollection I have of 'Dubya' is of the tall riding boots he wore, boots with a long dark blue stripe down the sides.

About Texas itself, the thing that impressed me was what the Texans had done regarding the relationship between universities and business, and commercialising research outcomes. We have adopted some of that thinking for biotech in Queensland. I was to meet Bush again briefly in Canberra during his 2003 visit.

Despite his pleasant manner, it would be hard for me to say that George W. stood as the greatest role model any leader could aspire to, whereas I found Tony Blair to be impressive as an individual and interesting as a politician. We met following the Centenary of Federation service in Westminster Abbey that was attended by the Prime Minister of Australia and all the state premiers. Blair talked of his friendship with Geoff Gallop and Kim Beazley, and the positive views he had about Australia.

When the premiers were introduced to the Queen after the church service, I put a lot of energy into trying to hide the fact that I had a bad cold. I tried not to share my germs with Her

Majesty; passing on my cold seemed hardly the right way to treat the Head of the Commonwealth.

What history teaches

Anyone who has given European history a cursory glance can see that the continent has had an insane past and has struggled to find a lasting peace. Those of us who grew up during the Cold War era lived with the constant threat of nuclear war. The thought of that used to scare the hell out of me when I was young. For a time, it was believed that there were individuals and societies who were contemplating the destruction of the planet as a legitimate choice in some mad political scenarios. I am more than glad that the present generation doesn't have this riding on its shoulders. Nuclear threats from so-called 'rogue states' exist, but back in the 1960s the tensions between the United States and the Soviet Union had led to a policy encapsulated by the acronym 'MAD' — Mutually Assured Destruction. As phrases like these have disappeared from the world's languages, I feel safer now than I did when I was growing up.

Some suggest that the end of the Soviet Union was an event bordering on the miraculous. I would say no, that its demise was due in large part to the actions of some extraordinary individuals. Sure, the communist system was imploding under its own contradictions, but who's to say what might have happened if the leadership of that system had fallen into further reactionary hands? Instead, the incomparable Mikhail Gorbachev came along. It's an honour for me to say I have met him; he came to Brisbane in May 1999. Although he is seen as a failure in Russian domestic politics, on the international stage he is someone who has made a difference to the history of the world.

Look at the times in which he was raised and the system he inherited; how frightening, how monstrous it was. Then, suddenly, it all ended. And to Ronald Reagan and Mikhail Gorbachev we owe a debt of gratitude for their considerable part in ending it. The world is still full of turmoil, yet the possibility of total annihilation is a much more distant prospect than it once was.

The humble and great

It's an honour to have met some of the greats of our times, but it is ordinary Australians, the citizens of this country, who inspire me most. Initially, my grandmother probably had the biggest influence on me, and I've mentioned other people along the way. It is often those who've been through the school of hard knocks and emerged intact who really drive things along. Usually they are nameless to me, but a bloke I met one day in Cairns has stuck in my memory. Coincidentally, his name was Keating — Kevin Keating.

A recovered alcoholic himself, Kevin was running a breakfast service out of an old home. Those going through hard times —

the down and outs, and druggies and drunks — could come in
and get their bangers and mash from him for breakfast. It was
early one morning when I met him, not much after 6.00 a.m.,
and it is not an exaggeration to say you needed a peg for your
nose in that environment at that time of day. But here was this
guy who had got himself off the booze, and he was out there
giving all those people a hand. He didn't want any recognition;
he didn't want anything at all; he was someone who knew what
it was like to be at rock bottom and he wanted to do something
positive.

In my book, someone like that is a great Australian. And
Kevin amounts to more than most of the political hacks I've
ever known. At the crack of dawn each day, he'd be up doing
his bit for his fellow man. A truly extraordinary individual.
Whenever you meet people like Kevin Keating, and there are
tens of thousands of Australians of his calibre, it is a privilege
that they will talk to you, that they will give a little bit of
themselves to you.

Having always enjoyed reading history, I know well that
history is always written by the winners, not necessarily the
most virtuous or on whose side justice might have lain. As a
society, I believe we should try to give thanks to the Kevin
Keatings of the world. I am pleased that today we have a system
of acknowledging Queensland's important individual
contributors by way of the annual Queensland Greats Awards.

I can attribute my love of history, at least some of it, to
another humble man, a retired farmer named Sid Townsend.

When I was a kid, my Nana took Sid in as a boarder. I can't remember when or why — people did that then — I can only remember him always being there. I don't think Sid had ever married. His main interest was books, which he loved and devoured. He must have read every book in the Atherton library, and he loved to talk. For hours we discussed world events — why Germany had lost World War II; how a nation as great as Germany had sunk into the clutches of a Nazi demagogue; China's future in Asia and the world, and what it meant for Australia; and the Brisbane Line, how we North Queenslanders would have been abandoned if Japan had invaded the Australian mainland. So it was Sid Townsend, an old retired farmer, who helped give me my love of history and maybe first sparked a political interest within me. He died in 1971, well into his eighties, when I was in first year at university. My step-grandfather died the same year; they had been great mates.

As a young person, I was able to make sense of things with a little help from my friends, and old Sid was one of them. My grandparents and Sid and I often talked of the Depression and the tough life that went with it. It was in answer to my questions that they would tell me what had happened, but they never complained or made speeches about it. Their attitude was that life handed you good and bad, and you just got on with it; tomorrow was another day. They also viewed helping one another as part of being a good citizen. They never glorified their helping each other, they just did it. And in doing so they exhibited the best Australian spirit. From them, and others like them, I get the greatest sustenance of all.

And last but not least, Professor Glyn Davis, Vice-Chancellor of Melbourne University, former Vice-Chancellor of Griffith University in Queensland and the first head of the Premier's Department from 1998 to 2001, after we won government. He provided the intellectual fire power for my dream of Queensland as the Smart State. A powerful mind, encased by humility and clarity, he taught me the full power of ideas forged into a vision.

Learning and giving back

You are never just a sponge for the ideas and spirit of other people. While acknowledging my debt to others, my own contribution, I like to believe, is a philosophical commitment to education that is probably stronger than some of my fellow leaders. It is certainly stronger than we have seen in the recent federal government, Labor or conservative. The other Peter Beattie contribution is inclusiveness, something I believe in fervently.

We are not here to ride around in limousines — that's easy, and it doesn't do anything to improve people's lives. I'm committed to good policy that produces good results.

FAMILIES AND SECURITY

Empowerment

Personal empowerment is important; financial security is important, as is personal responsibility. Like many people who didn't have money when they were kids, financial security has often been on my mind. My aspirations were not over-the-top — I wanted to own my own home with my wife, and to raise and educate our children; I wanted my kids to have the best education possible. My kids went to state schools for their primary schooling then did five years at private schools. I believe people should have that choice. Anyone who wants a religiously oriented education for their children should also have the option.

Returning to the issue of empowerment, I have always tried to ask myself, from the perspective of being in government, what can we do to help?

Employability

Governments can — and must — assist with the empowerment that comes with employability. To help a person in life, the best thing you can ever give them is education and training. Education is like a set of keys. From education flows personal growth; education and training give people transportable skills so they can protect themselves in the workplace. An educated population creates its own jobs and economic development, which in turn generate personal satisfaction and self-reliance.

You cannot promise ordinary working people specific jobs; what you can offer them instead is income-earning security. In other words, in times of change a person will have a job but not necessarily the one they've got now. Unfortunately, not enough of my union colleagues warm to this concept.

Let's encourage education and training towards employability. Once there is the opportunity of employment, a function of a healthy basic economy, then you have to have employability.

Financial security

Ultimately, financial security is personal empowerment. In order to have personal financial security, we have to encourage businesses to be internationally competitive and to have benchmarks that are international rather than purely domestic and/or state-based. Gone are the days of competition merely between Brisbane and Melbourne or Brisbane and Sydney.

Brisbane and Sydney are competing with Hong Kong and London. It's a global market now.

We need an export culture, an innovation culture. In order to foster these things, a government has to put in place the right tax laws and a degree of positive action.

Haves and have-nots — mind the gap

One of Australia's strengths is that, traditionally, there has not been a huge gap between the haves and have-nots. Of course there are differences, but we have a robust and safe society in which people are paid reasonable wages and work in reasonable conditions. Widening the gap is extremely dangerous. Let's look at the have-nots: if you have a significantly large underclass, then you have an unhappy group of individuals plus social problems on a wide scale.

It's worrying to note the considerable widening of that gap under the Howard government. In a statement to parliament on this subject, I quoted the findings of Professor Peter Saunders, the Director of the Social Policy Research Centre at the University of New South Wales, that between 1994–95 and 2000–01, the average income in the top fifth of the population increased by $111 a week. This is more than eight times as much as the increase of only $13 a week for the lowest fifth of the population. Professor Saunders said that although incomes rose across all sectors, inequality also increased 'particularly under the Howard Government'.[1]

Further on in my statement to parliament, I observed that I would hate to ever see Queensland follow the United States example. There, thousands of people are forced by economic circumstances to live in trailer parks, despite working at two or three jobs trying to make ends meet, while growing numbers of wealthier people live behind gated communities, shut off from the rest of the world in 21st-century fortresses. I place a high value on the fact that Queensland towns and cities are communities made up of people from all walks of life and where everyone is treated as an equal.

My government has been tough on the causes of crime and tough on crime itself — and crime rates have been falling in Queensland. But this becomes more difficult if Mr Howard's policies result in the gap between rich and poor continuing to widen.[2] Social dislocation will increase.

Corporate greed — not good

Although a side issue to the topic of the gap between rich and poor, there is also a problem with the discrepancy between the well-paid and the overpaid. I refer, of course, to those outlandishly high corporate salaries, the ones that run into the multiple millions.

As premier I am paid a salary with allowances in excess of $200,000, an excellent salary and better than most people receive. You'll hear no complaint from me on that score. It isn't that I aspire to match the CEOs and the many senior people in the private sector who are paid obscene amounts, but I query the inherent message of such excess. It's beyond my understanding why a chief executive walks away with a handsome package even if the value of a company's stock goes down; that's rewarding people for failure. This cannot be healthy for society at large, and the corporate sector and regulators need to take a good hard look at this.

In terms of the dollar cost to society, personal corporate greed is merely a drop in the bucket; yet it does have an impact socially, on morals and ethics. Such behaviour makes it much more difficult to encourage a culture of thrift and self-reliance, something that is also important to a healthy society.

Personal financial management

It appears that in education generally, scant time is devoted to the vital question of being able to manage your financial affairs. Budgeting, running households, not getting into debt — these used to be thought of as vital skills.

I'm all for trying to educate people to put away a percentage of earnings. I encourage my own kids to put away, say, ten per cent of their salary. If you have it taken straight out of your pay and invest it into a managed fund, you'll never miss it. Let it grow and become a little nest egg. When my daughter turned eighteen, I gave her a present in the form of some money invested in a managed fund; I put in a modest sum to kick it off for her. She knows that one day she will be able to do something with it, and in the meantime it is growing.

It is government's role, as I see it, to foster a culture of innovation and responsibility in personal finance. We have to teach people, even battlers and those who don't have a lot of money, to save that tiny percentage but to do it in a managed way. Broader issues are involved here, many ifs and buts, and I'm fully aware of all that. However, ensuring people have that bulwark of personal financial security is important. The younger they start, the better off they will be.

For a while now Australians have not been savers. Why not run a national campaign to turn that around, to encourage the idea that saving is a good personal practice, much like good personal hygiene? Clean your teeth, have a shower, put ten per cent of your salary in a managed fund. It's not that hard. Better that than hear people throw up their hands and say, 'I can't afford a deposit for a house, I've got to borrow everything.'

Forces exist, I know — like American interest rates, Australian debt and a poor balance of payments — that are so much bigger than any individual. And I appreciate that in Australia we have rising land values and it's going to be harder for our kids to buy a home. But we're changing in that, too. Renting is not the end of the world, provided you have a savings strategy in place. Indeed, there are a few economists and financial advisers who argue that you shouldn't buy property, but instead have a managed fund to which you add savings, and at the same time rent your accommodation (I don't agree by the way). Financial security can come in many ways.

Welfare and support

Although I espouse self-reliance, I am conscious that it is not always achievable. When people can't support themselves, government has an essential role to play.

In many people's minds, welfare is a dirty word, but it shouldn't be. When they downgrade welfare, politicians of the Right victimise those in need. This is not exclusively an Australian phenomenon, of course. Interestingly, in the USA the Democrat versus Republican welfare debate shares the hallmarks of the argument between our two main parties here in Australia. Although the language is slightly different, you have two opposing views on the fundamental question of who is responsible for people's wellbeing. Our conservatives seek to divide and blame when they run the line about welfare making life 'too easy' and taking away individual initiative.

The Labor Party's philosophy involves helping people in need. Of course, people have to take responsibility for their own lives. But some, for physical or mental reasons, can't. Everyone has the right to human dignity and a certain quality of life, so if someone is permanently wheelchair-bound or has a life-threatening illness, they are entitled to various forms of assistance. An individual whose life has been broken can never reclaim their self-respect if those in the broader community turn their backs. Dignity of life is a basic human value that we all have to uphold. Australia is a humane society. By and large our citizens feel people should be supported when they are in need.

A separate issue is the unemployed. A perennial fear in certain sections of the community is that there are unemployed 'out there' who could be helping themselves, but who are instead exploiting the system. The stark reality is that full employment is not achievable. Obviously I don't support the idea of anyone bludging, but there's no point stigmatising those whose luck has run out or who have never had any opportunities. My priority is to provide people with the right environment so they can help themselves. It's more productive to find a way to encourage those who are struggling and to support them in reaching their potential. That's why, for instance, we're promoting mature-aged TAFE programs in Queensland. And that's why we're offering apprenticeships and traineeships to people forty-five years of age and over. TAFE, adult, and other forms of education give people a life-changing experience that, if it does not lead to an immediately positive employment outcome, at least will lift their morale and make them feel better about themselves and their options. Instead of making individuals feel like victims, you've got to broaden their horizons and encourage them.

As for deciding who is entitled to assistance, this has to be based on need. Shirkers will always exist, but rather than tar everyone with that brush, let's use objective criteria to establish need and to weed out the unworthy. If someone is locked into substance abuse, then a rehabilitation program is called for. Aside from physical impairment or disability, if you have good health and you are capable, you should make a contribution to society.

How much should people in need receive? We have established in this country the idea of a living wage, and that should be the standard. You can't expect people to live in poverty.

Why are we one of the most harmonious societies in the world? I believe it's because there is not a huge gap between the haves and the have-nots — not that we should rest on our laurels about that. Also in our favour is that we don't have the depth of problems they have in some other places.

In 1985 I was in the United States as part of a political exchange program. At Dupont Circle in Washington I saw beggars for the first time in my life. It was December and winter; I saw them lying on subway grilles to keep warm. My jaw dropped. Here in the capital, shall we say, of the Western world — surely the wealthiest nation on earth — that seemed so wrong. Had it been India or drought-stricken Africa, I would have been less surprised. You could view this as a testament to my naivety at the time — although I was in my mid-thirties, hardly a kid — or you could say that I had grown up in a society where that sort of thing was anathema and that our people, through our governments, worked against such degradation. I prefer the latter assessment.

Sadly, the phenomenon of street people has emerged here more recently, too, but the sight of those beggars in Washington brought home to me that in certain fundamentals, America is an inconsiderate society. While I understand the American system and appreciate its strengths, it's still more dog eat dog than I would prefer Australia to be.

If you want a healthy, harmonious society you look after the people in need to ensure that if they can work, they get a job, they contribute. If this isn't possible, then the least we can do is look after them, and give them the human dignity that comes with being considered worthy of being cared for.

All members of society should be expected to use the abilities that God gave them in order to realise their full potential, and to maintain that by work and effort. That's what a community and a society is about. You don't ask someone to become a rocket scientist if they don't have that sort of capacity, but you encourage them to discover their strengths and to work to them.

From an early age, my children have all had part-time jobs because I wanted them to learn the work ethic. Each of them has worked at McDonald's. The boys have worked for Coles Myer part-time and other jobs such as 'outside' clerking for a law firm, while Larissa has worked in various restaurants. In the process they've learnt about money and how to manage it, they've gained an understanding of the value of work but the experience has also taught them how to interact socially.

Australia is currently suffering a skills shortage. Mums and dads should talk to their kids about skills training, including the trades. Apprenticeships can give a lifetime of job security and certainty.

Crime and punishment

Another way governments can contribute towards people's sense of wellbeing and security is to try to reduce crime and to appropriately punish those who do offend. If a government puts in place measures to encourage personal financial security and economic progress for families and individuals, it also has to safeguard people's hard work from acts of crime and violence. Proper justice has a very social function in this regard.

Crime and punishment are matters requiring careful thinking. You can't afford to be squeamish and back away from these things. Some of our views on crime strike me as wrong, and I've reached this conclusion only after a long period of research and discussion. It is my considered belief that sentencing and punishment should be broadly based. If you commit a serious crime, you do the time. I've always believed in the Christian philosophy that someone should be given another chance, and everyone's soul — no matter how evil — can be saved and redeemed. But what I have come to realise is that there are some sick people out there, such as incurable paedophiles, who cannot be redeemed. They are too far gone.

In my view, hardcore paedophiles who have breached the law and damaged the lives of children should stay in gaol. If their urges are uncontrollable, they should stay behind bars. If they can be declared safe by the experts, and rehabilitated, and have served their time then they should of course be released. But children are the most important element in any society. They have to be protected. My government has passed laws to make this philosophy a reality.

It is well known, or should be by now, that I have liberal views about personal behaviour. What two consenting adults do is entirely a matter for them; they're the ones who have to look in the mirror and weigh their own consciences. But I have no tolerance whatsoever for interference with children. I'm hard on it because it curtails children's ability to reach their full potential; it impairs their ability to learn, to be educated; and it scars them forever. In the worst cases, it absolutely ruins their lives.

We've had some disgraceful abuse cases in Queensland, as there have been in the rest of Australia. Nationwide, it's time to rethink our view on paedophiles.

Other kinds of sociopaths exist, pathological killers for instance, who also appear to be irredeemable. Outside of those few cases, people should be rehabilitated in prison, if at all possible, and then released.

At the risk of alienating some people, including those on my side of politics, I have no issue with building more prisons. We have built more in Queensland. When you take criminals off the street, the crime rate actually can go down; you discover that a small number have been committing a whole lot of crimes. These are facts of life. However, prevention is better than cure. Prison should certainly be a key part of our response to crime, but not the first response. We have to be tough on the causes of crime.

We've got to look at individual prisoners and ask, why are they in prison? Many have learning difficulties, many are not educated, some can't even write their parole applications. So what we do is try to educate and train inmates, equip them for the possibility of leaving prison and having another chance at life — at trying to be better citizens. With the exception of paedophiles, when someone's done their time and they've gone through the process, they are entitled to another go.

Mandatory sentencing is something I oppose. It's better that each court has the authority to pass its own judgment. Nevertheless, in Queensland we're tough on crime. The attorney-general has the right to appeal if they think a judgment is weak or too narrow, and our attorney-general has done that on a number of occasions. And if you commit an offence with over ten years' penalty, which is serious, you must serve 80 per cent of your time.

I don't believe in capital punishment. Too many mistakes are made by the law. And I would never want it on my conscience that there was a man or woman who has lost their life because of courtroom errors.

Since becoming premier, I have tried to put in place policies that nip crime in the bud and keep potential offenders out of prison. We've introduced positive parenting courses to give parents more skills and to learn how to give their children a go. We've put nurses into schools to help with getting kids off drugs or stop them in the first place. It is plain that the majority of crime is crime against property, and seventy to seventy-five per cent of that is drug-related. We have to do what we can to save these kids from drugs.

Our being tough on the causes of crime has brought results; in a number of key areas we have experienced the lowest level of crime for ten years.

There are twenty-six major offence types. Of those, twelve (almost half) have seen a drop in the rate per 100,000 people for the whole of Queensland for 2003–04.[3] (Comparisons for crime statistics can best be made by looking at the rate of offences per 100,000 people as this takes the population growth into account.) Essentially most of the major offence types have seen a drop.

These figures build on the trend of the past three years. They prove that while there is still work to be done, Queenslanders can be confident our police are making great strides in controlling and detecting crime, and providing a safe place to live.

Our policies of being tough on crime and tough on the causes of crime are resulting in many crime rates falling. In March 2005 the Queensland Police Service Mid-Year State-wide Crime Statistics showed a further decrease in crime rates, with significant declines in the rates for murder, attempted murder, sexual offences and weapons offences. The figures for

1 July to 31 December 2004 show that the murder rate dropped by 17 per cent, attempted murder reduced by 35 per cent, the rate of sexual offences dropped by 16 per cent and weapons offences were reduced by 19 per cent. The review also showed a drop in the rate of assaults by 2 per cent and unlawful entry by 10 per cent. The total rate for offences against people was down 4 per cent and the rate for offences against property was down 12 per cent.

These are the 'fear' crimes that result in old people barricading themselves indoors and in being frightened to go out. Unfortunately, they are also the crimes the media seize on and portray frequently and graphically in the news. So while the crime rates are going down, coverage of the actual crimes continues unabated and the perception that people are unsafe in their homes, in streets and elsewhere continues to worry them. The 1989 Fitzgerald Report showed all categories of crime had been rising for many years, but since June 1998 we have succeeded in reversing those trends. There has also been a general increase in clear-up rates by police.

The March statistics continued the sustained downward trend in the rate of most categories of offences over the last five years that was demonstrated by the 2003–04 annual review of crime statistics released in November 2004. Between 1997–98 and 2003–04 the rate of serious assaults in Queensland for every 100,000 people decreased from 297 to 285 — a 4 per cent drop. Armed robbery was down more than 30 per cent since 1997–98, robbery by about 28 per cent, kidnapping about

15 per cent, unlawful entry by more than 25 per cent and arson by about 18 per cent.

These figures were mirrored in the 2005 Productivity Commission Report, which showed that whereas there were 5300 victims of personal crime per 100,000 people in Australia in 2002 (up from 4800 in 1998, when the last survey was carried out), Queensland had the lowest rate in the country (4700 victims for every 100,000 people) and was the only state where the number of crime victims went down. The Productivity Commission Report also revealed that Queensland had the lowest rate for victims of robbery in the latest Australian Bureau of Statistics crime and safety survey — half the national average.

I believe we have the best police service this state has ever had. While the previous government promised an extra 300 police every year, it was only able to deliver an average of 200. But we have delivered an extra 300 new police every year, taking the size of the service from 6800 to 9800 early in 2005 — an increase of nearly a third in the size of the service.

Pride in a community makes a big difference in reducing crime and making people feel safer. Urban renewal — doing things like renovating houses and providing well-designed parks and recreational facilities — is another positive means of supporting families. Our urban renewal projects in various communities have re-injected pride in those places. In some suburbs where previously there was only Housing Commission accommodation, calls to the police dropped 60 per cent when we helped rebuild the suburbs.

Neighbourhood and family

When I was young, my grandmother was part of a genuine support network — as were most members of her generation. It was a functioning entity, incorporating aunts, uncles and cousins and long-term friends in the immediate vicinity, or at least not too far away. Neighbourhoods were places that could — and did — lend support. Many people today have never experienced neighbourhood in that way.

Family, too, has changed. Last century, or perhaps the one before, a much more supportive family system existed the world over. Nowadays it seems that only European and Asian families generally still maintain those old-style connections. With the erosion of that close connection in the broader community, what a lot we have lost. Taking our family as an example, Heather and I have been flat out in our respective work roles, and the raising of our three kids was something we have done on our own. Heather was the primary carer, and although there was some assistance from time to time, it was tiny.

In our society, when people become parents, almost overnight they urgently need an enormous range of skills, all of which their mothers and grandmothers were supported in developing when they had their own children. Ours is an ugly world in many ways, and there are huge demands all round. So the family unit is ever more isolated and pressured.

It's tough being a parent; it's tough being a kid. Thanks to media awareness, peer group pressure is stronger than it has ever been. Having — or not having — the latest designer clothes and so on can be a huge burden for adolescents, and even for younger children. As a group, the young enjoy accessing information; they revel in it. But as well as suffering from a general overload of useless data, they also have more access to challenging information — about alcohol, drugs, sex, and many other things. Teaching kids how to deal with all that is an additional challenge for parents. How do you cope with all that? Who helps you filter it or work out what to make of it when you don't have the support systems that used to exist?

I love my kids — all of them. No one gets trained as a parent, and all the text books in the world never really prepare you for the highs and lows of parenthood. I think there is only one golden rule — be guided by your love as you encourage and guide your children to reach their full potential. And when they are old enough, never be afraid to let them have the space to grow on their own.

I believe children do better at school if parents take a keen interest in their schooling. Larissa, Denis and Matthew all played sport at school and I always made an effort to attend their sporting and debating events.

We always encouraged our children to bring their friends home. From their early years with 'sleepovers' to their eighteenth birthday parties, their friends were always welcome at our home, and we got to know and like them.

Heather and I also learnt it is smart to drive your children everywhere. Eavesdropping on the backseat conversation with their mates saves asking a lot of annoying parental questions.

My children taught me the joy of the little things, and those are the memories I will hold until I die. Heather took a photo of Larissa, at about twelve months, sitting on the ironing board. She had the most magical smile — one of a child who was loved and very happy about it. Denis played centre forward in soccer when he was seven. His first goal after many attempts lit up his face. It was marvellous and unforgettable. Our third child, Matthew, is a gentle but determined boy. At eight he got it into his head one day that the other soccer team wouldn't score — he played fullback, a defensive position. He battled the whole game in a magnificent performance only to see them score almost on full time. The sad look of disappointment as he ran across the field to me at game's end almost brought a tear to my eye. In the end, it's the small personal things that matter in life. My kids taught me that.

To be perfectly plain, I regret not spending enough time with my family. A large part of it is that there simply haven't been enough hours in the day — not in the context of the things I have chosen to try to do in the political arena. Knowing how hard it is to manage competing demands in contemporary life has informed much of what I've tried to do in policies in this area.

Women's roles

Some still believe that a woman's place is in the home, but that sort of thinking sticks out like a sore toe; we're all equal. It is now widely appreciated that the work of raising children is best shared. Due to the demands of my job, I haven't done as much personally as I would have liked. Not only has Heather taken up the slack, she has also pursued her own interests and developed her career. She became a Doctor of Education, and she is now an Associate Professor in Nursing at the University of Queensland.

In the fact that Heather and I both work and have had to juggle our responsibilities to our children, we're a fairly typical couple. It's challenging in many ways, but we've grown together over the course of some three decades of marriage because each of us is having a fulfilling life. Having a partner who has their own ideas and appreciation of what's going on in the world brings intellectual stimulation and discussion to a relationship, making it strong. It's vital that your partner is able to perform in their own sphere and have their own respect, challenges and personal development — and that you can encourage and support each other's aspirations.

In late 2002, Prue Goward, in her role as federal Sex Discrimination Commissioner, put up a parenting support proposal, by way of a paid maternity leave scheme, to try to improve the situation for working women. Realistically, the way to achieve this is to provide tax deductibility to those employers who will pay. Having said that, I am all for retaining those talented people in the workforce. Having a baby doesn't entail losing your brain. It's crazy to have people in their best creative years effectively prevented from contributing to the workforce and the economy. We have to find a way through it — for the sake of families and individual security.

INDIGENOUS AUSTRALIA

Too long in the 'too hard' basket

Australia has had over two hundred years of failed policy with Indigenous Australians. For decades, governments have thrown up their hands and said the 'Aboriginal problem' is too tough to deal with. There have, of course, been plenty of negatives to feed this sort of defeatism. Historically, Aboriginal people were moved from their traditional lands and herded into communities which were and still are often extremely isolated. Dispossession wasn't restricted to the nineteenth century. As recently as 1963, when bauxite deposits were being opened up, the Queensland government evicted the community at Mapoon on Cape York from their homes, which were then burned along with the church. Palm Island, off Townsville, was used for many years as somewhere to dump troublesome Aborigines from all over

Queensland. Some 1600 people from forty tribes were sent there over the years.

The communities have had little or no employment, no future, no hope. Too many people have resorted to alcohol. Violence is one result; imprisonment is regarded by many young men as a rite of passage. Sexually transmitted diseases, rape and sexual assaults, including child abuse and incest, are all part of the tragedy. Drinking bouts late into the night mean children don't sleep and often don't go to school. Suicide rates among young Aboriginal men are six times higher than elsewhere. Alcohol-related death rates are more than twenty-one times higher than the Queensland average. Diets are unhealthy. Life expectancy is about twenty years less than for Australians who are not indigenous.

New leaders, new ideas

Now, at last, we are starting to see a significant shift, particularly during the 1990s, in Indigenous people's own thinking about their situation and the way forward. From the completely paternalistic scenario of forty and more years ago, we have moved to a point where, not only do Indigenous people want to take control of their own lives, they know they've got to make it happen themselves. Many powerful advocates struggled long and hard to establish this kind of attitude, individuals like the late Charlie Perkins, whose pioneering work others have taken up today. The views of the broader community have also shifted, I believe — few would dispute the rights of Aboriginal or Islander people to take charge of their destiny in the same way as any other individuals or group.

Noel Pearson epitomises the new style of leader. He is refreshingly honest about his own people's role in their affairs, including failures to take up the challenge. A handout mentality is anathema to him. Instead, he is determined to encourage self-criticism as part of moving towards true independence and proper self-management. Undeniably, many issues are yet to be tackled, not only in Queensland but nationally. Everything — from education and quality of life to the truly critical matters of health care, mortality and longevity — still needs serious attention.

Plotting a path for government

My government has taken an active and totally new approach to the affairs of Indigenous Australians, but I would be less than honest if I said our rate of progress is where it should be. The situation for many Aboriginal people is still a sad one. The prevalence of violence, domestic violence and alcohol abuse, including foetal alcohol syndrome, remains far too high. However, I am taking the long-term view, and I'm confident we are getting there — even if it takes twenty years before this story will no longer be such an unhappy one.

Governments have tried throwing money at problems in the Indigenous communities with discouraging results. After years of paternalism, it is clear that the only way to start tackling the problem is to enable these communities to write their own agendas.

Rather than focus on the negatives, which are still many and varied right round the country, I would like instead to detail some positive policies and activities we have put in place over the past few years.

Cape York Justice Study

The first step we took in establishing a new approach was to identify all the problems, then recommend how they might be tackled. In July 2001, Justice Tony Fitzgerald accepted my invitation to lead the Cape York Justice Study. His goal was to develop strategies that targeted the causes of crime on the Cape, focusing largely on community-based responses to widespread alcohol and drug abuse. He negotiated to work part-time on the study and refused to charge for his services. The reputation and integrity of Justice Fitzgerald lent the resulting study both standing and impact. Best known as Chairman of the Queensland Commission of Inquiry into Possible Illegal Activities and Associated Police Misconduct 1987–89, Justice Fitzgerald's outstanding career in law includes the role of President of the Queensland Court of Appeal from 1991–98. He also chaired the Commission of Inquiry into

Conservation Management of Fraser Island and the Great Sandy Region 1990–01.

Delivered in November 2001, Tony Fitzgerald's landmark report about Cape York justice contained a wide-ranging list of recommendations to help Indigenous communities develop and implement action plans to improve their lifestyles. While the report's focus was about government helping the communities to help themselves in tackling the causes of crime, it stressed that the attitudinal and behavioural changes which are essential to the survival of communities and their children's future can best be brought about by the people themselves.

To paraphrase the report, it said the government should support and assist each community to create action plans that will allow for alcohol management; law enforcement and relevant justice arrangements; strategies for improved educational outcomes; strengthening families; and strategies and partnerships for improved health. But the report also said that it was impossible for community leaders to do that at the time because:

> The breakdown of social cohesion, the tacit acceptance of alcohol abuse and violence as normal and the reinforcement of lowered self-esteem in the communities compounded by their inability to interact successfully with the complex structures and processes which accompany Government activities, have produced a self-perpetuating cycle of poverty, tragedy and despair.[1]

Tony Fitzgerald identified three goals for future government intervention: a simplified, integrated government approach; the development and implementation by each community of action plans; and ongoing monitoring and evaluation of results.

He suggested that funding should be allocated on a competitive basis with incentives provided to communities on measurable indicators of social wellbeing such as health, education, reduced breaches of the law, reduced levels of violence, and community support for programs aiming to improve local conditions.

Other recommendations included strict enforcement of laws relating to the supply of alcohol; the provision of safe places for women and children in every community; the provision of violence-prevention programs; a public education campaign to enhance awareness and promote the value of education, including awareness of child-rearing practices that enhance school readiness; and the enforcement of laws regarding school attendance.

So serious were the problems identified by the report that I felt the state government should take immediate action. I arranged a meeting for the following day of all Queensland Government department heads to start considering the recommendations and to report within two months on how government actions and resources could be refocused to meet the challenges. I asked the Minister for Aboriginal and Torres Strait Islander Policy, Judy Spence, to head a team to work with

Cape York communities in dealing with the report and its recommendations.

Before the end of the year the Aboriginal and Torres Strait Islander Commission and the federal government agreed to join forces with us to help Cape York communities help themselves. Given the central tenet of Tony Fitzgerald's report is that the change essential to the survival of the communities is best brought about by the people themselves, it seemed imperative that those concerned own the change to ensure it is sustainable. The next stage was to involve the people of the communities in taking on ownership of the recommendations that they accepted. And government had to work out how it would deal with the process.

The domino effect of alcohol management plans

In April 2002, after consulting about 700 people, I tabled in parliament 'Meeting Challenges, Making Choices', a report pledging reforms to legislation and policy to address the alcoholism and violence in Indigenous communities. Our report adopted the bulk of Tony Fitzgerald's recommendations, while a number had been modified after careful consideration of community responses. We have to effectively counter the devastating impacts of alcohol abuse and violence before we can address health, education, unemployment, and law and order issues.

The new approach included:

- Enabling the government to transfer canteen licences from Indigenous community councils to Community Liquor Licensing Boards. This ended the potential for conflict of interest, identified by Justice Fitzgerald, between councils running and managing canteens and their responsibilities relating to welfare and law and order.
- Giving a legislative basis to community justice groups in remote Indigenous communities, and empowering the justice groups to declare dry places in their communities.
- Imposing strict conditions on hotels and roadhouses near Indigenous communities — including banning alcohol sales to taxi drivers; barring licensees from holding a patron's bank access cards; prohibiting the sale of liquor in containers of four litres or more; and restricting the time of day that take-away liquor may be sold.
- Strengthening and expanding community justice groups, and giving them the power and protection of legislation for the first time.
- Working smarter with the communities to exploit economic development opportunities.
- Working harder to address the symptoms of alcohol and substance abuse: for example, through the

establishment of a rehabilitation service hub in the Northern Peninsula Area.

- Intensifying the war against 'sly grog' by tightening up teamwork between communities, police and liquor licensing boards.

By mid-2003 I was able to report that from Aurukun, Doomadgee and Nupranum we were receiving reports of a better quality of life, especially for children and women. In Aurukun, which was the first community to implement strong alcohol management strategies such as restricted- or dry-area regulations, the number of alcohol-related injury presentations to the community health clinic had already fallen. In the same community, school attendance rates improved from 38 per cent in 2002 to 50 per cent in 2004. Significant improvements were also evident in Pormpuraaw, Kowanyama and Lockhart River.[2]

Alcohol-related crime and injuries in Aurukun have dramatically decreased. Queensland Police statistics showed alcohol-related offences decreased by almost 40 per cent, from a monthly average of twenty-three recorded offences in August–December 2002 to fourteen offences for January–May 2003. At the same time all offences — whether alcohol-related or otherwise — dropped by 25 per cent, from a monthly average of forty-two offences to thirty-one offences. When comparing the five months before and after alcohol restrictions, there was a 25 per cent fall in property offences.

The health statistics are also encouraging. In the three months after introduction of the plan, presentations for alcohol-related injuries at the community health clinic fell by 73 per cent when compared to previous months. The number of presentations for injuries caused by assault dropped by 57 per cent for the same period.

By November 2004 all but two of the nineteen communities — Cherbourg and Palm Island — had alcohol management plans in place, with Cherbourg reaching the final stages of its planning process.

Radical improvements in community life were never expected to occur overnight because — sadly — the decay has been occurring over generations. But signs of improvement are filtering through.

Between January and June 2004 the changes included:

- A 48 per cent reduction in the monthly average of alcohol-related presentations to community health services in Aurukun, Doomadgee, Lockhart River, Mornington Island and Pormpuraaw.
- Funding for four child health workers, two women's health workers and two new alcohol, tobacco and other drugs positions on Cape York.
- The appointment of a full-time officer to work with Aurukun youth to reduce abuse of substances such as petrol, and to tackle youth crime.

- The appointment of a Suspected Child Abuse and Neglect team coordinator for Cape York–Torres Strait.
- The implementation of economic development projects such as a nursery and market garden at Mapoon; the upgrade of the Napranum concrete block plant; and several Indigenous tourism projects including Silver Plains camping infrastructure, the Umagico camp ground, Wujal Wujal Walker Family Tours, and projects at Chuula and York Island.
- Nineteen visits by government 'community champions' — departmental chiefs designated to work with particular communities.
- Five negotiation table meetings — forums for government and communities to come together to identify and agree on ways to address local priorities.
- Funding to support an additional 100 youth support coordinators in order to provide prevention and early intervention in schools.
- Additional funding for sporting and recreational facilities and programs.

We are now strongly focused on education, housing, and reviewing the alcohol management plans after they have been in place for more than a year. Indigenous parents, elders and community leaders share the government's desire for better results for school children. Like them, we want the young ones to be better prepared for work, further studies and job training.

Importantly, while the alcohol management plans address supply of alcohol, the government is developing a strategy to better manage the demand for alcohol and other substances.

Three years on, my government is encouraged by improvements in some aspects of community life, and we are more determined than ever to build a brighter future.

What particularly delights me is that school attendance and food sales have improved, because this means kids are better nourished, more alert, and education has improved. In other words, kids are getting a real chance at life. Communities are said to be quieter; children are at home at night instead of on the streets; and more and more young mothers are taking walks with babies in prams.

Of course, the situation is still far from perfect, and communities such as Palm Island present major challenges. But finally a real start has been made towards improving the lives of Indigenous Australians.

Employment and education

The government's Partners for Success strategy aims to improve education and employment results for Aboriginal and Torres Strait Islander Queenslanders. This recognises that our state education system has not met the needs of the majority of Aboriginal and Torres Strait Islander students and that we have to do better. The document itself marks a new era of cooperation, consultation and partnership between government,

Education Queensland and Indigenous Queenslanders to create the best sort of future possible for all children. Partners for Success is aligned to the government's Cape York Partnership Plan.

In employment, we have worked up a variety of policies and initiatives to increase employment and retention rates of Aboriginal and Torres Strait Islander people in Queensland. We now have, for instance, the Indigenous Employment Policy introduced in May 2001, requiring state government building and construction contracts in Indigenous communities to employ a minimum 20 per cent of local Indigenous people. Indigenous people have also benefited from programs under the 'Breaking the Unemployment Cycle' initiative, and by 2004 are receiving 14.9 per cent of overall public sector apprenticeships, traineeships and job placements. The government has also put in place ten employment and training coordinators across the state whose job is to work towards increasing retention and completion rates of Indigenous apprentices and trainees.

In Cape York, five employment and training coordinators have assisted with the development of forty-one community training plans. An economic development initiative called the Cape York Partnerships, which the government started two years ago to address crippling levels of unemployment and welfare dependence, has led to more than fifty full-time, part-time and seasonal jobs and training positions in communities including Wujal Wujal, Napranum, Mapoon and Mossman Gorge.

Examples include a mudcrab and fishing enterprise in Mapoon, jointly funded by the Queensland and federal governments, which is proving to be a big hit in providing fresh seafood to locals on the west coast of Cape York. The Napranum community has established Nanum Tawap Ltd, which runs a portfolio of businesses, including a concrete block plant. The Queensland Department of State Development has injected $148,907 to upgrade the plant, which supplies Comalco. Private sector partners such as Comalco, a commercial fisher and a retailer have helped make a number of Cape York enterprise opportunities possible.

In July 2001 we introduced the Aboriginal and Torres Strait Island Public Sector Employment Development Unit, to be responsible for working with agencies to achieve a minimum 2.4 per cent of employment for Indigenous peoples across the sector in 2002. By June 2003, 2.6 per cent of the public sector was Indigenous.

Native title

On the subject of native title, I have personally been keen to put in place a 'negotiation not litigation' philosophy. And this philosophy has underpinned a native title agreement that ends the journey for land rights begun almost twenty years ago by the late Eddie Mabo over the Murray Islands in the Torres Strait. In 2001 Federal Court Chief Justice Michael Black, in a special sitting on the Eastern Torres Strait island of Dauar, ratified the agreement and granted native title rights to that and the island of Waier. This was a very important event, not only for the specific islands in question but for Indigenous Queenslanders generally, boosting morale and indicating that ours was a non-obstructionist government when it comes to their rights.

On the subject of land use, the state government gained the agreement of four land councils to join with us in consulting communities about a model for state-wide native title agreement. Our aim? For the first time in the nation's history, we wanted there to be a single process for all types of exploration activity; in other words, we wanted to work around the difficult high- and low-impact distinctions contained in the Native Title Act. In 2003 we passed legislation to further assist exploration activity in Queensland's mining industry, legislation that was supported by Indigenous interests as well as the mining industry. Without a doubt, Queensland today leads the nation in Indigenous land use agreements.

Artistic and cultural work

For a long time now we have marvelled at the artistic expressions of our Aboriginal people. Increasingly, artists from the communities have been recognised and their work sold, collected and made available via galleries and institutions. As Indigenous art has become more widespread and visible, it has also moved and inspired hosts of other Australians.

To expand and develop Indigenous art and artists, I established a unit with the business and trade area of government — not arts — to encourage local artists. We have sponsored art exhibitions in Sydney, Berlin, Düsseldorf, London and Washington. My government also presented *Story Place: Indigenous Art of Cape York and the Rainforest*, an exhibition of the distinct artistic styles of the Cape York region. We have taken Queensland artists to the world, like Shaun Kalk Edwards, Craig Koomeeta, Rosella Namok and other members of the Lockhart River Art Gang, whose works are now highly sought after by leading international collectors and dealers.

Two calendars highlighting this art have been produced for wide distribution to business, scientists and political leaders. A publication called *Gatherings* depicting Queensland Indigenous art was produced and widely read. We also established *Virtual Gatherings*, an online resource for the promotion and marketing of Queensland Indigenous art.

I personally use *Gatherings* and the calendars as gifts around the world. Indeed, when the Commonwealth Heads (CHOGM) met on the Sunshine Coast, the Queensland Government used it as an opportunity to promote our artists. For example, we commissioned eight Aurukun master carvers to cast traditional sculptures of plants and animals in aluminium and bronze for the meeting.

It seems that we have only recently understood the importance of focusing on these achievements and getting serious about showcasing the work of Queensland's Indigenous artists to the world. It is my intention that the government continues to support, and do what it can to further develop, Aboriginal and Torres Strait Islander artists and their industry. Their work in this area already makes a contribution towards economic viability for Indigenous communities; we now need to focus on its capacity in some cases to provide economic independence. This is all about personal empowerment.

The truth is simple — if we can't beat the grog, it will devastate another generation of Indigenous Australians.

The 2004 federal election saw the ALP's vote drop in many communities. This is a direct result of our alcohol management plans. This is putting pressure on the state government but we will not back off. Unless we fight the grog problem, the rest of our strategies will fail.

I'm personally determined to continue with this strategy whatever the political cost. Heather spent her early years in an Indigenous community — at Edward River (Pormpuraaw). Her father was an Anglican priest there. We are both committed to making a difference for Indigenous people even if the results won't be obvious until I am long gone from politics.

THE AUSTRALIAN
LABOR PARTY

ALP longevity

Having been around for over a hundred years, the Australian
Labor Party is the oldest of Australia's political parties. It has a
huge and complex structure, and anyone who believes he or
she can get it to change easily is living in a fantasy world. Then
again, just as it has some deeply rooted traditions, it has also
undergone all sorts of evolution. As recently as the 1950s, the
ALP had a White Australia Policy. The ALP's support of that
can be explained to some degree in that there were concerns
about employment opportunities for Australian workers in
among the more base prejudices about colour. But if the Party
suddenly turned around today and pledged support for a
White Australia, it would have to immediately write its

obituary. I've been in the ALP for a long time. At the end of the 1970s, after we lost the 1977 federal election, I saw the Party go through the Button Committee inquiry. This was a committee appointed by the ALP National Executive to examine the ALP's national platform and plan for the future. It was headed by Senator John Button, future Hawke minister. Ours is a Party that has grown and matured over time, and that process is ongoing. Similarly, the union movement is facing significant challenges, because the nature of work is changing.

If I were to put together a sermon for the Party on a nationwide basis, it would go something like this: the average Australian worker has been through more change than perhaps the political parties themselves, and therefore the Labor Party, representing those very same people should know that change is inevitable, unavoidable and necessary. We have to implement policies which help Australian workers develop skills which enhance their employability and give them more certainty in an uncertain world. The only way to do this is through a strategy to enhance skills and employment flexibility.

Reforming the Party

After a period of uncertainty it's heartening to see that a process of renewal in the federal ALP is well underway, with with a number of former stars heading to the backbench. For all that it goes through occasional periods of turmoil, it seems

to have an uncanny, almost organic ability to bounce back —
it's as though the ALP possesses a kind of immune system.
After Mark Latham became leader, we witnessed an initial
revitalisation and then a devastating election loss in 2004.

John Howard's 2004 victory demoralised the ALP nationwide.
What's more, Howard now controls both Houses, courtesy of
four Coalition senators from Queensland. The result was a real
shocker in this state. The ALP only won two of the six Senate
seats and six of the twenty-eight House of Representatives seats.
In Queensland we now have Liberal–Labor voters who vote
Labor at a state level and Liberal at a federal level. The days of the
rusted-on voter have gone.

The nationwide result for Labor was so bad that a win in
2007 is difficult at best. What went wrong? Howard out-
campaigned us. His negative ads on interest rates scared the
hell out of the electorate and we didn't answer them and we
lost. It was that simple. Sure there were other reasons at the
fringes, but that was the chief reason.

To win we need good policies, great candidates and a
winning campaign. Our candidates were mixed, our policies
were fair but lacked economic weight, and we lost the
campaign; that is it in a nutshell.

To win the next federal election the federal ALP needs a clear
strategy. The return of Kim Beazley as leader meanwhile gives
the ALP at least a hope. The Premiers supported a change of
leadership from Latham to Beazley in the interests of boosting
the overall chances of the Party.

The Labor Party in Queensland was a basket case in the 1970s before the Reform Movement took hold. It had no policies and although there were some good people, there were not nearly enough of them. Today, in the federal sphere, the ALP is developing policies and trying to put them before the public, but more need to be done.

At the time of writing, things are far from perfect. One outstanding matter is the selection of candidates. Nationwide, the Party still has too many less-than-productive members. A method of selecting and presenting a balanced array of good candidates strikes me as being a fundamental necessity. Unfortunately, the practice of putting up hacks because they're somebody's mate is still going on. Nevertheless, things are better than they were. There was a time getting good candidates to run was the exception rather than the rule. At least in Queensland we're now endorsing good people most of the time.

However, poor candidates in two federal seats in Queensland cost us dearly — indeed, one cost us a seat. In the regions in particular, the quality of the candidate can be the difference between winning and losing. The electorate is smarter than some in politics understand.

Not for a minute am I suggesting that it is only the ALP that gets it wrong. In 2003 we saw the phenomenon of Malcolm Turnbull going around trying to stump up a few hundred people to take over a local Sydney branch. It would be interesting to know what practical positives he was offering the people of Wentworth electorate other than his status as a high flyer. This sort of thing is pretty unsightly, and more importantly, alienates individuals from the political processes. He won in 2004 and good luck to him. However, the sooner he rises through the Liberal ranks the better for the ALP.

Factions

Factionalism is a facet of the ALP that tends to get a lot of publicity, much of it negative. But lest anyone think factionalism is solely the preserve of Labor, may I remind them that the Libs, too, have their factions, traditionally the 'wets' and the 'dries', and the Nats and Libs are perhaps just two different conservative factions. The important point to make is that the Labor Party is not owned by anyone in particular and it must never be just the plaything of the factions.

ALP factions exist to delineate ideological argument, but they also exist to achieve a result once a consensus has been reached. Let's not beat around the bush — factions and sometimes faction leaders can be an impediment to change and good Party management. When you have factional leaders who can rise above their factions to think of the Party, then you get a good Party, and you need that before you get a good government. Those who are self-interested, navel-gazers or plain greedy for themselves and their mates will always damage the Party. In Queensland today, while traditional factionalism has an influence, it doesn't play a big role in the Labor government — and when it does play a role, it is usually positive.

I've now got to the stage where I think factionalism has at best a medium level of value. Not of no value but of medium value. I could be critical of the faction system because I've personally experienced the harsh side of it and I've seen its negativity and short-sightedness. But I have to say I've also seen its strengths. A particular instance of the factions being useful was after the rorting scandals, when I went to the Party and the various factional leaders and said that we had to do X and Y. To their credit they all stuck with me. The Party in Queensland held itself together and was strongly disciplined in cleaning out the people who had been misbehaving. In other words, when the blowtorch was put to our belly on that occasion, unity within and among the factions proved extremely effective.

When the Labor Party is united and heading in the one direction, it's unbeatable. When it's not all heading the same way and is divided, it never wins. One thing the ALP's factions need to do is help the federal Party plan its strategy for the 2007 federal election.

Parties only win campaigns if they have good candidates, good policies and a good campaign. We need to start work on all three right now.

I often joke with Heather that this book should be titled *Politics: The Art of Managing Egos*. And that's what the Party has to manage federally. Before anyone gets too excited, I admit I'm not short of ego either. But this is not about me; it's about the ALP being able to prepare itself to be a credible alternative government. We weren't under Mark Latham; we can be under Kim Beazley.

Let's start with candidates. The federal leader and key Party powerbrokers should encourage some old stayers to retire — and give some younger members a go. I admire Senator John Faulkner for standing down from his leadership position. Some other Party players should leave parliament altogether. If the Party could endorse at least one promising future 'star' from each state — in a winnable seat — the signal would be powerful indeed. Powerful to both the electorate and to the Party. And let's not forget the Senate. Some of our favourite Senate hacks could go now; let the change begin mid-term. Build a momentum for change. Show we are serious.

But it's in the marginal seats that most care needs to be taken. We must get a factional consensus for excellent candidates who have proven links into the community, not drinking habits with their factional mates. We have to have the strength to reject mediocrity. Only the best candidates will get us elected.

Secondly, on policy, we have to develop and explain our economic strategy well before the 2007 campaign or the Coalition will re-run its fear campaign from 2004 and we will lose. We should highlight the Hawke–Keating economic track record; people have forgotten it. We should be proud of it. If we haven't established sound economic policies and sold them to the Australian people prior to the campaign, forget it — we'll lose again.

Thirdly, we're not bad at campaigning but could be better. We should run a mini campaign on our economic strategies in early 2006 just as if it was the real campaign, explaining our strategies. Television, radio, newspaper ads, the lot. We should spend the money selling our vision for Australia and it should be a vision for a smart Australia for the next ten years and beyond. But you would expect me to say that! I'm happy for our Smart State strategies and policies to be stolen.

At this point I have a confession to make. Like many Party people I was devastated by the 2004 federal loss. Queensland provided four of the senators which gave John Howard control of the Senate and twenty-two of our twenty-eight federal seats. How embarrassing!

For a brief moment I thought about running as a candidate in a marginal federal Liberal seat in 2007. At the end of October 2004, after the election, I was in Adelaide and Perth selling Queensland. Party members there were shattered by the federal loss and it started me thinking. Later, back in Queensland, I attended a political wake at the Abruzzo Club at Carina for my friend, Con Sciacca, who had just narrowly lost the seat of Bonner. Wayne Swan and Kevin Rudd were there, together with over 200 Party workers and supporters who were looking for hope. I wanted to help make a difference.

But this rush of blood to the head passed just as quickly as it had arrived. I have the best job in Australia as Premier of Queensland and I love it. My commitment is first and foremost to Queensland. Besides, I haven't finished cementing in my Smart State strategy yet and at fifty-two I'm probably just too old to be part of what could be a six-year plan. I will assist the federal Party where I can — but they have a lot of work ahead of them.

The Party-policy interface

To me, the development of the policies that the Party takes to the people at election time has to happen not only within the Party itself — whether that's at branches, the national conferences or any other official forum — but between the Party and the Australian people. Good policy is like a well-woven rug — each thread has a place in relation to each other thread, otherwise the thing doesn't make sense as a whole. And because we are talking about a big warm rug for a whole room, not just a doormat — the conservative side specialises in the doormats — you could say it needs a bunch of skilled people all working harmoniously towards the one goal.

The question of how much government policy in Queensland is a reflection of Cabinet's priorities and how much has come from the Labor Party is an interesting one. It might be better answered from a historical or analytical standpoint; my own viewpoint is way too subjective. If a person is a product of environment, upbringing, education and experiences, then there is no question that the ALP is a key part of my experience — and that of my ministers too. I am a

Labor Party person through and through, and I live and breathe the Labor Party in the sense that I know what it stands for — first and foremost for fairness — and I love the Party because of it. I have contributed to policy debates; I have listened to other people's contributions to policy debates. Although I've given my bit, I've taken from this process probably more than I've put in.

Through a multitude of conferences, through talking to individual Labor people old and young, I have listened to people all along the line. I could not have achieved much without the input of other ordinary Labor Party people. And they include trade unionists, conference delegates, people who have gone to conferences just as observers, someone you might pass in the street and who doesn't necessarily have a self-interest agenda — ordinary Australians. The Queensland Government takes pride in being to some considerable extent a conduit for the desires, the demands, the will and the interests of ordinary people. In that regard, the Labor Party epitomises what I believe about education and about equal opportunity and fairness.

Like any politician, I'm not short of ego but I know the source of the ideas that I passionately believe in and the vision that I have. And without the Labor movement and all these people it would be nothing, it would be a shell. And a very hollow one at that.

A criticism sometimes levelled at me is that I'm merely a populist: 'Beattie's only giving the mob what it wants to hear.'

I beg to differ. I try to use talk-back radio to explain what I believe. Perhaps, in the sense that I want to help develop and then reflect a vision of a better life for ordinary people, I'm something of a populist. Perhaps the fact that I actually like people and enjoy talking to people also makes me slightly populist in style. Yet I don't always do the 'popular' thing. The Queensland ambulance levy is, for instance, controversial, but its practical effect is that people won't die on the side of the road because the ambulance service isn't properly funded. Among other initiatives in our state, the Suncorp Stadium in Brisbane wasn't initially popular, nor was the Goodwill Bridge. They are now.

The only legitimate model for the relationship between a political party and the people is the one where you represent the broad view and have the people's support for it. If, on analysis, you find that you have been wrong and have to change some long-held favourite idea or policy because it was ill-conceived, then you explain to the people that you had it wrong and then try to rebuild the relationship. Sometimes the media won't give you credit for that; they'll call you a jellyback, or some other name, and accuse you of a backflip, but when there are higher things at stake, so be it.

Too often in politics it is made almost impossible by both political parties and media commentary for politicians to accept that they are wrong and apologise. I have been criticised over a number of years because I am prepared to accept it when I realise I have made a mistake, to admit it, say I am sorry, fix it and move on. We need more flexibility, more generosity of spirit in politics and an acceptance that none of us is perfect; the last person who was perfect was crucified. It is impossible for politicians to get it right all of the time and we should say so. And the media should give them credit for it. Instead, the political process and the media see this as a sign of weakness which undermines the leader, and too often leaders are forced to try and stubbornly fight or defend a position which is almost untenable and wrong. We need to greatly change the culture of Australian political parties, the political process and the media to allow our leaders to be what they are — human.

Vision versus management

Before anyone can presume to 'lead' politically, they have to find out what the people want from their leaders and indeed from politics in general. What I've found is that communities want you to have a vision, they want you to have some belief in what you're doing, and they want you to be fair dinkum. People have no time for shysters and shallow spin-merchants. I believe that the experiences of the Queensland ALP, where in recent years we have aimed for openness and creativity, and we've been trying to be positive, are worth learning from.

I passionately believe that political leadership should be used to bring people together, to heal divisions and renew society. Australians are sick to death of brawling politicians. Paul Keating was one of the sharpest parliamentarians in

Australian history, but many Australians, particularly women, seemed to dislike his antagonistic performances during Question Time. Most Australians want politicians to work together for the sake of the country. Some political 'sophisticates' may regard that as a simplistic interpretation, but that's my reading of our society.

Sadly, it's not that hard for a leader to appeal to the dark side of the soul, as Hitler demonstrated only too well. They'll inevitably strike some kind of chord. But in the end, that negative style of leadership is destructive. It's harder work trying to appeal to people's better selves, but many are the great leaders who've done so. Gough Whitlam did. He may not have known a lot about economics but he aimed for the high road. The likes of Whitlam, Chifley and Curtin all left something for the future, as did Hawke. Because he reformed the economy, I think history will judge Hawke well.

I can't say the same for John Howard, for we have to ask: what is the Howard legacy going to be? He has done some good things in government and I have personally worked well with him, but when the test comes on the visionary initiatives, he is more often to be found taking the short-sighted view. From the Queensland perspective we can see this in his government's foot-dragging over stopping tree-clearing, and over a lack of strategies for a smart vision for Australia. I doubt whether John Howard possesses the kind of vision this country needs for the next ten or twenty years. (Maybe four-year terms would help him.)

As a politician you can be either a manager or a visionary. Some people might replace the term visionary with statesman; substitute your own term for that person who has imagination for the common good and is prepared to lead their society there. Having a manager is fine, but where a manager gives you today, a visionary gives you today and tomorrow. And that's a big difference. A visionary provide the tools on behalf of their society so that the society can go about creating its future.

The last federal government in Australia to have had the sort of visionaries this country needs was the Hawke–Keating government. That government initiated reforms in economic and other areas, and set us up for the forthcoming period. The Howard government has worked with that inheritance, but has not built its own; it has not provided new reforms for the future.

The Howard government has occupied itself with far less critical things. You might ask, for instance, how much time has the Howard government spent on appointments? It has politicised every aspect of senior appointments. It's not necessary to do that; my government doesn't. We've appointed former lord mayor Sally-Anne Atkinson, former National Party premier Mike Ahern and other political conservatives to important positions in various fields. These individuals were appointed because they are good people who possess the talent required. On the odd occasion I have appointed to certain positions people whom I don't personally like — indeed I have had to say to my staff, 'This is the right person but, please, I don't particularly like them personally.' If you surround yourself solely with like-minded people — clones — you're not serving the community.

Alternative leadership

The biggest problem currently facing the federal ALP is that the Howard government has clearly used the uncertainty that has arisen as a result of international terrorism. At a time of fear, the message is put about that a strong leader like John Howard can keep Australia safe. To me this is sheer manipulation. Many people who really don't like him have been convinced by Howard that in such a time of trouble, he is the man of the hour, the one who can protect us. That strategy works brilliantly politically because people subjugate their legitimate and real concerns — about healthcare, education, nursing homes, homelessness, family services and so on — to the overriding concern of security. Security is the policy-free zone where the government is getting free kick after free kick. The only real path of action left open to the federal ALP is to pursue positive policies on the fundamentals, to expose the dishonesty of the government, and to show the people of Australia that they are a viable alternative party.

The ALP and the states

One of the vital roles the ALP has played in the history of our country is its role in the affairs of the individual states. After

all, it is at state level where most of the practical things that
affect people on a day-to-day basis are run — water, electricity,
roads, hospitals, schools and so forth.

Apart from our routine contact with each other by phone or
other means, we state and territory leaders — currently all of us
belong to the Labor Party — get together formally at meetings
of the Council of Australian Governments (COAG) at least once
a year. COAG has replaced the old Premiers' Conference and is
the peak inter-governmental forum in Australia, comprising the
prime minister, state premiers, territory chief ministers and the
president of the Australian Local Government Association
(ALGA). The prime minister chairs COAG.

The official role of COAG is to initiate, develop and monitor
the implementation of policy reforms which are of national
significance and which require cooperative action by Australian
governments. Medicare and education top the list; among the
other regular agenda items are Indigenous affairs, guns,
terrorism, National Competition Policy, gas reform, electricity
reform, water reform and reform of Commonwealth and
state/territory roles in environmental regulation. Other issues
come up through the system, such as Ministerial Council
deliberations, international treaties which affect the states and
territories, or major initiatives of one government, particularly
the Commonwealth, which impact on other governments or
require the cooperation of other governments.

The private dinners hosted by the prime minister at the
Lodge on the eve of the formal COAG meetings are pleasant,

informative and constructive occasions, and I enjoy them. I can picture my first pre-COAG Lodge dinner — the Prime Minister talked warmly about Steve Waugh and cricket, and meanwhile Bob Carr warmed to a subject that fascinates him and in which he is learned, the American Civil War. Bob has always been great to work with. He has a fine intellect and is a person of engaging charm. My only concern about him is the state of his knowledge about football — he knows far more about American history and the Battle of Gettysburg than he does about league or union or AFL. He and I have our annual State of Origin bet where, if Queensland wins, the Queensland flag flies over the Sydney Harbour Bridge, and if we lose, the New South Wales flag flies over our new Suncorp Stadium.

As I write, the level of cooperation among these Labor leaders is unprecedented. We share a personal warmth and respect. Geoff Gallop and Mike Rann and I met years ago. I also enjoyed a long association with the late Jim Bacon. Although he did unwittingly drop me in it one time. Heather and the kids and I were holidaying in Tasmania and we went round to Jim's place to say gidday. Shortly afterwards, he was addressing a group of tourism operators and happened to mention my visit. When this was reported at home, I copped it for holidaying away from the world's greatest tourism destination, Queensland. Jim didn't mean to cause any harm, and the hullabaloo quickly abated, but he certainly warmed up my Tasmanian holiday. Steve Bracks became Premier of Victoria in 1999 and has impressed me as a fellow visionary who wants to build for the future of his state. Gallop, Rann, Carr and I also cooperated to try to persuade the AFL to host preliminary finals outside the MCG when non-Victorian teams are in the ascendency. To date we have failed. Understandably, Steve Bracks has held the Victorian line.

State and territory leaders pulled together on the issue of stem cell research, which allowed COAG to develop a national approach. Without that level of cooperation, the stem cell debate would have fragmented; there would not have been a national decision, and that would have been embarrassing internationally for Australia. We have also managed to work solidly and soundly with Prime Minister John Howard. We used to have many disagreements, but lately we have arrived at some significant achievements. That Labor leaders could work with a Liberal prime minister surprised some of the cynics. I would argue that it's about time.

Queensland has cooperated to an enormous extent with the Commonwealth. My government has worked closely with John Howard's government on gun control, water, industry, stem cell research, and on many other issues. We cooperated early on tree clearing before the National Party eroded Commonwealth dollars for the plan.

Some of my Labor colleagues may have difficulty understanding this, but I have worked hard at having a good relationship with John Howard. Whatever you may think about John Howard's politics, he is hard-working and his attention to detail when he is focused on an issue is impressive.

During the GST meeting in Canberra, the Prime Minister and Treasurer, Peter Costello, presented the federal government's case. Howard was across as much detail as the Treasurer and, on a couple of occasions, more so. On a personal basis, Howard is not reluctant to make a call on an issue. When my government was trying to save the Australian Magnesium project in Queensland from voluntary receivership, he left a federal Cabinet meeting and rang me to confirm the Australian government's position. We agreed on a joint approach, and the risky bid went ahead. We may argue the toss on many policies but we have at the same time managed to arrive at a working relationship.

John Howard and I talked about the GST deal at the Lodge one night and we reached agreement about funding for Queensland. The COAG deal on the GST meant Queensland accessed the GST money a year earlier than originally planned, and that meant that Queensland was better off. However, there is no Howard vision for biotechnology, for Information and Communication Technology (ICT), for major events, for infrastructure, for real research dollars, education or health reform. I hope this term the Prime Minister will work on his legacy.

The states and a vision for Australia

The Olympic Games in 2000 confirmed Australia's place on the world stage. Our sporting figures, our actors, our tourism images and our relaxed attitude to life make us one of the most 'liked' nations on earth. I would like to add another layer to our reputation, and this is of Australians being respected for our intelligence.

In 2003 Steve Bracks and I attended BIO 2003, the world biotechnology conference in Washington. Bracks, Bob Carr and I had reached an agreement in June prior to the conference to highlight our states to the world as a bio hub, promoting a Smart Australia. Bracks and I started work on this a year earlier at BIO 2002 in Toronto. The agreement is called the Australian Biotech Alliance. Extraordinary things are happening in Australian universities and research institutions. The historic agreement initially only included Victoria, New South Wales and Queensland, and it put aside state rivalry and joined our forces to promote Australia's biotechnology and pharmaceutical industries to the world. It now covers all Australian states and at Queensland's insistence, New Zealand.

At BIO 2004 in San Francisco, four premiers — Bracks, Carr, Rann and I — were present, along with representatives from Western Australia, New Zealand and the Commonwealth, for the announced expansion of the Biotech Alliance. Together we aim to build on Australia's position as having the sixth largest biotechnology industry in the world in terms of the number of individual firms — now approaching three hundred. The combined Australian biotechnology pharmaceutical industry employs around 35,000 people and turns over around $12 billion. The private sector spends $450 million a year on research and development, and the public and non-profit sector around $900 million. Biotechnology plays a major part in developments ranging from cochlear implants, to diagnosing cancer, to new forms of DNA matching. It involves developing new products using living organisms and biological processes.

In Washington in 2003, the Queensland Government was able to announce a raft of major projects and discoveries in biotechnology:

- Human trials were underway at the Royal Brisbane Hospital into a protection method for deep vein thrombosis (DVT).
- A natural alternative to traditional antibodies for dogs was being developed by a Queensland company.
- An agreement between the Townsville-based Australian Institute of Marine Science (AIMS) and the US National Cancer Institute in Washington DC was reached allowing marine life in tropical waters of the Great Barrier Reef to be used in research which may lead to a cancer cure. If a drug is found, AIMS will be part of a potential US-billion-dollar-a-year venture. The opportunity is worth about AUD$100,000 a year to AIMS.
- A Brisbane-based security software specialist was helping pioneer a futuristic identity system for the United States Department of Defense. The company won part of the US$1.2 million contract to build the Smart Card access system.

- Another Brisbane-based company formed a new strategic partnership with the US to develop high-tech diagnostic monitoring tests for race horses.
- Plans for a hub for semi-conductive research activity were underway.
- Funding for a Queensland company developing a new class of antibiotics for fighting infection by so-called super bugs such as golden staph.
- Funding for the University of Queensland to detect testicular cancer, and to create a more effective system for air traffic control.
- Funding for the sugar industry to develop new products, such as pharmaceuticals and biodegradable plastics.

At BIO 2004 in San Francisco I announced nine projects to receive almost $42 million funding in total from the state government:

- $2.2 million to the University of Queensland to expand the Queensland Hypersonic Testing Facility Centre in Brisbane and Toowoomba.
- $2.52 million to the Queensland Institute of Medical Research to establish a Queensland Viral Testing and Product Characterisation Centre in Brisbane.
- $8.1 million to the University of Queensland to establish a Queensland Preclinical Drug Development Facility in Brisbane.

- $3.5 million to the Queensland University of Technology (QUT) to establish crop development facilities at Ormiston and QUT's Gardens Point campus in Brisbane.
- $9.5 million to the University of Queensland to establish a Centre for Advanced Animal Science at Gatton.
- $3 million to the Mater Medical Research Institute in Brisbane to support cancer and other disease research.
- $5 million to the Queensland University of Technology to establish a Medical Engineering Research Facility.
- $5 million towards the development of a Queensland Clinical Trials Network to provide a one-stop shop for national and international companies that want to conduct clinical trials.
- $3 million towards the establishment of a Centre for New Foods which will research and commercialise foods for better health.

The push for biotechnology is also a means to reverse the brain drain and indeed provide a brain gain. My government has funded universities that lead, or which are significant partners in state-linked Australian Research Council Centres of Excellence. Such centres not only attract renowned scientists and researchers from around the world, but they create employment opportunities and enhance education skills here in Australia. This century will be the century of biotechnology. Following the

Agrarian Revolution, the Industrial Revolution, and the Technological Revolution, we are now in the early stages of the biggest revolution of all, the Biotechnology Revolution.

Biotechnology is too big a step into the unknown for some people. My approach is to take off the brakes and go like the clappers. If we are not part of the Biotechnology Revolution, we will be left behind. Australia will become just a beach, maybe a lovely beach, but a beach nonetheless. Our children and grandchildren will miss out on the jobs of tomorrow. It is critical that we use our collective brains to secure Australia's future, and it is in central issues such as this one that we recognise the value and importance of the ALP and the contribution it can make to the health of our nation. That's why I say to the Prime Minister that we need an Australian vision for biotechnology. The states are doing their bit, but the Commonwealth is dragging its heels. Beyond that, Prime Minister, we need a long term vision for Australia!

Participation

Extra efforts are needed to encourage people to take an active interest in our democracy. My worry about politics and political parties is that ordinary people don't want to be involved in them. Membership numbers go up and down, but there hasn't been a huge growth in membership of any major political party for a long time. The ALP is the oldest party, and we probably have the biggest membership, but people have got to be inspired to join. One reason will be when we allow them access to real power. Some might see this as dangerous. But that danger is the only way that you'll get people to join the Party, and they won't ultimately be able to make a positive difference unless they're in it.

Is it such a big deal if we don't persuade enough people to join political parties? It's a huge deal, because otherwise the field is left open to the extremists of the Left and Right. And if such types sense that a political party can provide them with a free soapbox, they will take the opportunity to push their own narrow and sometimes just plain offensive line. In this I'm talking of the broad spectrum of the population, not just the Labor Party Left and Right.

Generally, the only people prepared to put up with what they see as the boredom of going to all the branch meetings and so on are diehards obsessed with peddling points of view rather than doing the hard work of practical politics for practical outcomes. Ordinary people don't stand much of a chance against the ideologically pure, the factional warriors and the instant experts on everything. They may want to contribute to a broad policy direction but they are thwarted by people who have personal agendas and who mainly want to sound off about things. This is a real problem in representational politics.

For the ALP, the challenge is for the power brokers to put themselves second and the Party first, to remember that they have the honour of influencing the future direction of the nation. Attitudinal change is vital. So, too, is having the right people. I've always believed that you can have the best system in the world but if the people who are operating that system are self-serving or they're second rate, then the system won't work properly.

As Sir Max Bingham, the former Liberal Deputy Premier of Tasmania and head of the CJC used to say, so much of politics comes down to personal character, personal commitment, and to personal integrity. I totally agree with him. You've got to have the best people with the best vitality and the best intentions. At the same time, I'm not making a case for purity and perfection. Nevertheless, I do believe we have to give a chance to those people who actually want to do things, who would like to improve the world and improve the lot of their fellow Australians.

Of course, in the real world there are people who hold positions of power and who will fight tooth and nail to hang onto them. There are also people who like to control, just as there are those who are prepared to be controlled. That is unhealthy for any democracy. The Labor Party in Queensland made the choice — the only reasonable choice open to us — to move the recalcitrants out of those positions through a combination of better policies and genuine and greater support. Had our Reform Movement not done its darnedest to rid the Party of such types, Wayne Goss would not have won in '89.

As to showing integrity, there is the excellent example of Neil Batt, once a Tasmanian, who found it a very difficult thing to support intervention in Queensland. But in the end he did it. People like him actually believed in the Party. Neil, as ALP National President, had the courage to vote for and support the removal of the old executive to pave the way for a new future for the Queensland ALP.

You may well ask: what do political parties hold out for young people? Fewer and fewer young people are joining political parties; why would they want to? It's a big problem. A depoliticised society is a dangerous one. But why do so many young people feel so alienated from political parties? We have to figure it out and do something about it.

I also have concerns about how some media report politics. My fervent hope is that in the course of their education, our young people are being encouraged to test the statements they hear in the media and make up their own minds about who's fibbing and where the truth may lie. Australians are not mugs. They are perfectly capable of looking at leaders and working out what they stand for.

A NEW QUEENSLAND

A culture of openness

Queensland has had good governments, in the sense of active, achieving administrations, and it has also seen drearily conservative governments. And while there have been good premiers on both sides, in my view, the excellent legacy of T. J. Ryan wasn't picked up again properly until Wayne Goss. My government has continued it just as vigorously. The first of the new style, progressive governments came in with Goss, although some people see him, and me, as 'progressive conservatives' in some aspects. But we have both overseen more open and socially responsible governments.

Without being egotistical, I can confidently assert that I do have a clear vision for Queensland — who would want a premier who didn't? The people who work with me know my vision and direction, and I'm blessed that they share it.

Looking back on this government to date, we have achieved some tremendous positives. Some arrived in the short-term, some in the medium-term, that is, up till 2005, and there are further objectives and goals to be achieved in the long-term.

Overall, there has been significant and positive change in the political culture that we have in Queensland. The kind of change I'm referring to began when Wayne Goss made street marches legal. People protest on the street, they protest outside Parliament House. As someone who himself demonstrated against Joh, I find it healthy — democratically speaking — that there are now people who demonstrate against me on various issues. And I stand by their right to do so. A group of dairy farmers came and demonstrated against my government a while back — as they did against the federal government, for all sorts of reasons. In Joh's day they would all have been arrested. Today our response is, 'You are welcome; feel free.' At our Community Cabinet meetings, people can come through the door, sit down across the table and talk to my ministers and me in person. Indeed, five hundred farmers rallied against our tree clearing laws at a recent Community Cabinet meeting in the western town of Charleville. That's what it means to open everything up.

New politics

To some extent, Australian politicians are constrained by the parliamentary system, the bear-pit model of combative and adversarial behaviour. But I'm firmly of the belief that you can rise above it. What I advocate is 'new politics'. I've previously shared my ideas about being tolerant, inclusive, forgiving, and not getting down in the mud where your opponents and others might like to see you — that is 'new politics'. It's about trying to rise above the worst aspects of political behaviour for the good of society. So, we don't go in for name calling. New politics is about doing constructive things, developing policy that will improve people's lot, and rising above the gutter stuff.

I don't always get it right. Despite my best intentions I do sometimes become annoyed by shouts, insults, interjections and untrue allegations. The result is that I occasionally say something in Question Time that I later regret. Overall, however, I have tried to stay positive. And I have tried to keep my government focused on the positive. I believe that the record in Hansard, and the tone of our ministerial statements generally, reflects that focus. That's new politics in practice.

Old-style politics, by contrast, was all about exploiting weakness and being adversarial. For decade upon decade in Australia's chambers of political debate, all kinds of damage was inflicted without heed to collateral damage to individuals, the party or other organisations. Take the example of Paul Keating. His capacity for bruising, old-style adversarial politics was a strength up to a point, but then it proved to be a weakness. For a Paul Keating style of politician, you can never stop watching your back, even once you have left politics. If you are habitually oppositional and are only ever on the attack in parliament, how do you operate, let alone win hearts and minds among Australians?

Old politics was also about appealing to prejudice. It was around 1987 — less than twenty years ago — that Russ Hinze boasted about how he'd left school at twelve and that he'd gone to the university of hard knocks and that's what counted in Queensland. Only one or two members of that Cabinet had a university degree, and the Nationals all seemed proud of the fact. Those sorts of old destructive attitudes have largely disappeared, and good riddance, too. Ultimately, we need a balance of education and experience.

The big picture

Never have I run my premiership, or this government, like a dictatorship. As for style of government, I strive to operate a consensus model but at the same time I try to clearly identify our long-term, non-negotiable goals. We've been prepared to stand firm on tough decisions like enterprise bargaining with unions, for instance, all the while trying to be fair to our workforce. The Queensland Labor government is focused long-term. We have ten-year and twenty-year strategies. Education, health, multiculturalism, the environment, our commitments to Indigenous affairs — all these feature prominently in our long-term vision.

The important thing is to get a good decision for the state, for the people. And if you are prepared to drive the process that leads to a good result, you will be afforded some respect, which is always good for the soul.

At the same time, we all know that not everybody's particular view can be put into action, and in the end I have to take a position. But I don't sit down and ruminate like an oracle then announce my decision. Ninety-nine point nine per cent of the time the Cabinet has talked the matter through, looked at the background ideas, thought about the different options and arrived at a consensus; in other words, logic wins.

Becoming the Smart State

'Smart State' embodies the Queensland vision we are working towards. It means using ideas, creativity and innovation to build on our strengths and create new opportunities; it is a positive state of mind. This government wants to promote the idea of doing traditional business smarter, running industry smarter, developing new industries, being innovative, thinking about the world, increasing exports, jobs, and thinking about where we are and where we can go in the future. That's the energy of change. Smart State was considered to be something of a joke when it started; it's not any more.

Even the Queensland Government's corporate logo has been revitalised — we've moved away from those old, stylised, mock-British coats of arms to something much more modern; it's all about change, and there are steps you have to take to get to the long-term. Rather than adopt strategies that last just long enough to get ourselves re-elected, we have instead opted for long-term strategies to benefit Queenslanders years down the track, when Peter Beattie and today's generation is long gone.

I regard it as vital to go beyond what's been thought of or planned or already exists as policy and program and try to imagine what sort of world we would like to have in ten years' time. In education, I want a world where kids start school earlier and stay at school longer; one in which greater numbers of young people go to university and to TAFE, and where more of them go into apprenticeships and traineeships. I would like to see better literacy levels, high numeracy levels, more tolerance and much more commitment to multiculturalism. In education, we've already changed the state from being a laughing stock to being regarded as one of the smarter places in the nation, and we're building on that.

In the economic sphere, I want us to value innovations and exports as well as trade, which is a key part of the Queensland economy. I encourage our businesses to think globally, to have a broader view than just Queensland and Australia, to think about our region, travel to our region, try to be better educated about our region and, in turn, encourage other people around the world to be educated here. In other words, I want us to have a very broad tolerant society which has an energy about it. Smart State is about a state of mind that leads to these sorts of outcomes.

I can't give an exact definition about how far we are along the Smart State road because I'm not quite sure where the road will end. Indeed, the whole concept of Smart State is that it shouldn't end. Meanwhile we can note that the Queensland Bioscience Precinct has more bioscientists than any other centre in the Southern Hemisphere. Smart State has caught on. Plus we have 5000 people working in aviation who didn't have these jobs six years ago, 2000 people working in research and 9100 working in export education. Queensland is changing for the better. Once we were a rocks and crops economy with a little tourism thrown in. Now, after spending $2.4 billion on science and research over the past seven years, we are all of that but much more. Our economy is broader and our advances cover everything from biotechnology to ICT to film.

The results are dramatic: in the last six years, exports have grown by 24 per cent to earn $30 billion a year and high technology manufactured exports have grown by more than 50 per cent in seven years. And ICT employs 56,000 people and earns more than $850 billion a year in export income. Our economy has radically diversified.

There are still individuals who are committed to a know-nothing mentality — to beer and bugger education. And then there are some who fit in to both camps, backward-looking and yet slightly forward-looking, too. But overall, Queensland is changing dramatically for the better.

Some of the signs are purely symbolic. For instance, Queenslanders who need new number plates are given a choice between a Smart State one and a Sunshine State one, and some fifteen per cent have opted for the 'Smart State' type. To me, that suggests that a growing number of Queenslanders are happy to identify with this vision. I believe Queensland can achieve many of its Smart State goals by its 150th anniversary of statehood in 2009.

Change in the social climate

Gradually Queenslanders are embracing more enlightened social policies. Our anti-discrimination laws are some of the most progressive in Australia. In our schools we have also made significant advances. In areas of social policy we are as progressive as New South Wales and Victoria. I was Chair of the Parliamentary Criminal Justice Committee that recommended the decriminalisation of homosexuality between consenting adults. The vote went four to three Labor versus conservatives, and Goss implemented it. De facto relationships can now be same-sex as well as different-sex; the same superannuation entitlements apply in all cases, ditto WorkCover entitlements and inheritance entitlements. The world has not been turned upside down because the law allows that homosexuals be treated as equals.

The Anti-Discrimination Act now prevents vilification. We have laws against vilification on ethnic grounds, which I promised the ethnic community, and we also have laws against vilification on sexual grounds. In a free and open society, you obtain the rich mix that comes when all sectors are allowed to have ideas, to contribute from their own unique perspectives and activities.

Plenty of people opposed these changes. My government and I copped a hard time as a result. I had some angry meetings with various people; one time, a group of two or three hundred in the Executive Building gave me a belting about anti-discrimination, challenging the definition of spouse, and so on. But I believe Australians generally will give everyone a fair go and they'll judge them on whether they're a good person or whether they're a bastard. And people can change their opinions. National Party member Vaughan Johnson is a perfect example of an individual who's had his own little conversion on the way to Damascus. He was the Deputy Leader of the Opposition in the National Party who, when we gave gay people rights under domestic violence legislation, said that if Labor MPs did not vote against the legislation, 'Jesus Christ will strike them dead in the end.' Since then he has softened his stance to the extent that he has indicated he'd have a beer with homosexuals as long as they didn't discuss their sex life.

On advancing rights and opportunities for women, our record speaks for itself. I've been a strong advocate for affirmative action, and our parliament has more women than any other in Australia. I was brought up by a strong woman who was fully able to run her own show; I'm more likely to be thrown by women who are uncertain or indecisive than independent women with robust views. The third most senior

minister in my government is a woman: Anna Bligh, the
Education Minister. She was on the Cabinet Budget Review
Committee in our second term.

The bush

Among the Beattie government's achievements, I like to think,
is the development of a whole new and better relationship with
the regions and the bush. Like other parts of non-metropolitan
Australia, the outlying areas of Queensland have had and in
many cases still do have significant issues to get through. This
latest drought has had an enormous impact on rural
communities; there are issues with communications, as the
continuing debate over what do with Telstra shows; and many
others debates lie ahead. But most turn on the question of
what is economically viable and what isn't.

To date, the bush has gone through a lot of change yet in
some parts there is resistance to change. As blasphemous as it
might sound, the Australian bush, too, in my view, has got to
be part of the global system. For instance, if call centres can be
anywhere now, they can just as easily be in the Australian bush.
Early on, few could see the value of, or wanted to support, an
inland railway like the Adelaide to Darwin railway, but now
everyone can see the potential economic benefits.

Over time mechanisation both on the farms and in
transport has altered life in the bush, and people have opted
out. Families with young kids, in particular, have left the bush

for education and other reasons, and often they don't want to go back. But new opportunities are opening up; primary producers are diversifying or reinventing themselves. Take the green, or organic, approach to growing food, whether it's beef or other primary produce. Japanese and European markets, and others, are demanding 'clean green' food and are prepared to pay good prices. Again, huge adjustments may be involved; quality may be valued over quantity, for instance. But there are plenty of new ideas.

The term globalisation — I'd rather there was another word for it — is like a red rag to a bull for certain people, yet globalisation represents opportunities for primary producers. We've got beef into Egypt, Vietnam and China, places that never before took it. And India's opening up right now.

Tourism is another huge opportunity for the bush, and the Queensland Government is mindful of its potential; the development of heritage trail networks is one example of how we are fostering growth in that sector. The bush can look at possibilities other than the traditional activities; things like call centres and new tourism can mean positive inputs to the economy of the bush. Innovative tourism can present fresh and interesting outback experiences, such as dinosaur fossils and trails, or the chance to view the stars in a new way (as at the Cosmos Centre in Charleville).

And then there are the enormous benefits that could accrue, as they did in the past, with a renewed push to encourage migration out into the bush and the regions. I don't think it's unreasonable to require new arrivals to spend, say, a couple of years outside the capital cities. Places like Cairns and Townsville have sufficient infrastructure to be able to support a greater number of immigrants, and would in turn benefit enormously in all senses from having them there. Obviously people are not going to want to go to a particular area unless there are jobs and opportunities, and you can't expect people to go to somewhere just because it's there. But we can be strategic and create incentives and environments which will have a positive pull for people.

In a way I'm really only advocating what happened here fifty or sixty or seventy years ago in the towns of North Queensland, where Italian and Greek and other immigrants made a tremendous contribution. I believe in welcoming more migrants to Australia, just as I believe in multiculturalism. I think we should continue to have a modestly large but sensible migrant intake, based largely on the skills that can be contributed to Australia.

Safeguarding our land and water

Although we've improved out of sight, my heart sinks when I go to public places and see that people have left their beer bottles and rubbish all over the place. Why should it be that hard to put rubbish in a bin? To me there's an indisputable link between what people do in their backyards and land management practices. You wouldn't put your rubbish in your bath, so don't throw rubbish in the creek. We Queenslanders have to continue educating ourselves about these things. Just as we have to have respect for each other as human beings, we have to have more respect for our physical world. Don't bloody well burn down the rainforests by being irresponsible; don't pollute our environments. Having said that, among young Australians I find a greater respect for the environment than there is among my generation.

We all have to wake up to ourselves about what we do with this fragile country. The state of Queensland's land and water is hugely sensitive. Both are critical resources and both are at risk. To protect the soil we've brought in restrictions to tree clearing, trying to ensure that the land isn't further degraded. This has been difficult politically and has cost us votes in certain quarters. As to water, we still need to educate Australians about our usage. Although ours is an arid country, as a nation we're extravagant with water. Perhaps because most of us live on the coast we have become blasé?

My Cabinet has spent more time talking about water and sustainability issues than any other single question. And it is a huge problem for us as we grow; indeed salinity is an enormous problem. More desalination projects are on the agenda, as is better management of our rivers. This is not a Green issue so much as a survival issue. And sooner or later we have to accept that the only option is sustainable development; without sustainability, we are lost.

One way we are meeting the water challenge is by bringing in charges for water. We have water meters in the city, and we are also now charging people for use of the river systems. Frankly, it's the only way to get people to say, 'Hang on, I'd better be sparing in the use of water.' And I am committed to a sensible, balanced water pricing policy. Sadly, if you don't highlight the scarceness of water by charging, unpopular as it is, then people won't appreciate that it truly is in short supply. Any farmer will tell you how vital water is and how much it is under threat.

Regarding open space and green space, we've implemented the Regional Forest Agreement. As mentioned, 425,000-plus hectares will become protected for future generations — that's also about respecting the environment and letting it have lungs to breathe. And also as mentioned earlier, we have decided that we will end broad scale tree clearing, with or without federal government support.

Queensland's future

Australia is moving north. Every week, well over a thousand people move to Queensland from interstate and overseas. Our rate of economic growth in 2003–04 was 3.9 per cent. The national growth rate, excluding Queensland, was 3.6 per cent. We are rapidly becoming the engine room of Australia and we are certainly the land of opportunity. In a hundred years Australia will be a different country, one in which Brisbane, Cairns,

Townsville, Weipa, Darwin and Perth will have a much greater role because of their geographical location. My prediction is that this state will become the California of Australia. Any business in Australia that does not have significant investments in Queensland will, in my view, be left out.

In the history of our nation, Victoria and New South Wales have had dominant roles, and they will continue to be significant, but Queensland is the future. In twenty years from now it will be bigger than Victoria in population terms.

Already it is eminently possible to set up a business in Queensland — with one of the best lifestyles in the world — and enjoy comparatively very low international cost structures. All this is on offer in a state with a multicultural workforce possessing skills and education. And we now know full well that our competition is in New York, London, San Diego, Hong Kong, Beijing and Tokyo, not Sydney and Melbourne, and we have long since adjusted our frames of reference accordingly.

One of the proudest achievements of this government has been the construction of the new Brisbane in partnership with Brisbane City Council. We have rebuilt the heart of the city. I'm referring to the Goodwill Bridge, extensions to the South Bank, the Roma Street Parklands and Suncorp Stadium. We are also working on a learning precinct at the Gona Barracks. We are building a new art gallery, extending the library, and using the river and its banks in a way that is unprecedented.

Brisbane has become the most liveable city in Australia, and one of the most liveable cities in the world. The sheer attractiveness of the city has become a major 'pull' factor for people from interstate and for those looking for economic opportunities. It is helping us attract business investment and is drawing new executives in areas like biotechnology, IT, export education and aviation.

Queensland was once the redneck joke of Australia — not any more. The Smart State strategies have changed that. But Queensland will continue to need to change for the better. And politically there will need to be ongoing renewal of people, policies and institutions.

We will continue to push Queensland to the world, rolling out more of our Smart State reforms such as the extra year of pre-school in 2007; getting fifteen to seventeen year olds to either be at school or in training, ie earning or learning; and continuing to develop a culture of creativity through the richest literary prizes in Australia and creative incentives in drama, multicultural photography, and the Arts. It's an ongoing process.

This is our future. This is the Smart State in action.

AUSTRALIA

Counting our blessings

In the aftermath of incidents like 11 September 2001, the Bali bombing, the recent bombing of the Australian embassy in Indonesia, the SARS epidemic, the war in Iraq, all the terrorism around the world, and the tsunami disaster of 2004, the world seems ugly and scary. In that context, you appreciate just what a lucky country Australia is. Still, when I am asked whether I am optimistic about the world, my reply is yes. On balance, and especially considering the numbers now inhabiting the planet compared to a hundred years ago, I think the world is becoming a better place.

Media attention has contributed to this progress. If television had been around and had focused on World War I, say, as much as it did on Vietnam, that nightmare would not have gone on for four and a half years and the butchery and slaughter might not have run into the millions as it did. In my view, something as immediate and accessible as television exposure would have dramatically foreshortened the whole tragic affair.

Looking out

Australia has a role to play in the world, not only for the fact that it is a 'middle power' but for the reason that Australia has traditionally been respected among nations. We should guard that respect and that independence in whatever we do. And while Australia has to be careful to distinguish its own stance, we do have to have allies like the United States and Britain. These relationships have been important historically and will continue to be important into the future.

However, while our relations with the US and Britain should be a key part of our international relations, it should not be to the exclusion of our Asia-Pacific neighbours, especially Japan, Korea, China, Indochina, India, Singapore, Papua New Guinea and, yes, Indonesia.

We are a modern, multicultural nation but we're also part of Asia. Given the fundamental fact that so much of the world is unstable, we need to forge strong partnership links with others in our Asia-Pacific neighbourhood. Australia has come to be well regarded, even in Vietnam and places where we've been in conflict. There is recognition that we are not an imperial nation and that we do have a cultural attitude of trying to treat everybody fairly. We have a history of looking after people both here and overseas — via aid — wherever we can. Australia's billion dollar aid package towards tsunami relief cements our position. (Queensland, by the way, has committed $10 million to help — our highest amount ever to any disaster relief effort.) We should never lose these values.

Occasionally, Australia demonstrates that it is a separate sovereign nation that judges issues perhaps a little differently than others. That streak of independence is important to our self-esteem as a country and also for our credibility in the world. At the present I don't believe we are seen as being as independent as we should be.

The two biggest achievements John Howard can claim for his prime ministership are gun control and East Timor. Australians have cause to be proud of what the Prime Minister did in East Timor, make no mistake. I went over soon after the Indonesian military left, and from what I saw with my own eyes, I say that with some conviction. That bit of independent action — standing up for East Timor — was the right thing to do. It would have been so easy to have acquiesced and let the injustices continue. Thankfully, we didn't. By the same token, that doesn't mean we have to get involved in everyone else's backyard. Where our neighbours are concerned, let's judge each situation on its merits and chart our own course.

Having a proper and decent response to refugees and asylum seekers is another thing we shouldn't shy away from. If people are genuine refugees, we have an obligation to look after them appropriately. Given the many crooked practices going on, like the people-smuggling trade, the Howard government did the right thing in sending a clear message. What I don't like is the way the federal government runs the detention centres; I take issue with the delays, and with the way women and children are treated. By and large, the administration of the detention centres is a shambles; I'd like to see a total overhaul of this policy. The position on refugees and asylum-seekers taken by the Labor Party both in the caucus federally and at the 2004 National Conference is spot on. Previously, Howard outmanoeuvred us. I'd like to see John Howard taken to task for his mishandling of both the *Tampa* and the 'children overboard' incidents, and for going to war in Iraq without UN support. It's a shame the Prime Minister won't admit the reasons for going into Iraq turned out to be wrong. Any objective assessment of the Howard policy shows it was based on faulty foundations. He should tell the truth about Iraq and *Tampa* and the 'children overboard' lie. It was clever politics, very clever wedge politics, but it was also a lie. History will not be kind to these lies.

First of all, the situation in Iraq should have been handled through the UN. Of course nobody wants to see weapons of mass destruction in the hands of an unstable regime — if they even still existed after the first Gulf war — but the response should have been UN-developed and UN-delivered. It is obvious now that there were no weapons of mass destruction in Iraq. Interestingly, Tony Blair and George W. Bush, as drivers of the push into Iraq, have met great criticism for the absence of such weapons, but not John Howard, their supporter. If we were all misled into going to war, let's now assist Iraq in developing a democracy, preferably through non-military aid. In such a classic crisis, many of us would like to see an independent Australia making what are obviously its own decisions.

If the UN had been part of the Iraq push, the mess today would be easier to fix — not easy to fix, just less focused on hatred of the US. Yes, both John Howard and George Bush have won elections post the Iraqi war, but they both await the judgment of history.

Australia and the international economy

Responding to the impact of internationalisation or globalisation on our economic situation is the next real challenge that we should be addressing as a nation. Of course, overseas factors affect us at every turn; we're part of the global market. What happens on Wall Street, Dow Jones and NASDAQ does affect Australia, whether we like it or not. State governments are impotent against global market forces; even national governments don't control the agenda in the way they used to. The American economy has had its troubles, too, especially if you look back at that country's experiences in the early '90s. Its economy now appears to be in the recovery part of the cycle; nevertheless, in the great home of free enterprise there is still economic uncertainty. Japan's economy, too, has had a rough ten years and the government has been trying to restore the banking sector with only qualified success. The truth is that governments around the world, especially those in the small-to-medium economies like Australia where they have opened up their economies, are at the whim of market forces like never before. We need to rise to the challenge. We need to be nimble as an economy, making sure, for example, that we increase our exports so that our other fundamentals don't falter.

So what do we do? Forget trying to fight globalism; go with it. Let's have knowledge-based industries with international benchmarks; let's compete with New York, Tokyo and London. We have to develop a stronger global outlook, and that's why skills and training are vital. If we can make people employable Australia-wide, in the end we make them internationally employable.

As a country of slightly more than twenty million inhabitants, we either choose to be internationally competitive or we'll be left behind. Right now, North-East Asia is acquiring tremendous economic power. Korea, Taiwan, China and Japan represent some thirty per cent of the world's capital. India too is quickly awakening from economic slumber. At one time, we defined ourselves in terms of our distance from Europe, but no longer is Australia's geographical location a disadvantage. We are on the doorstep of the biggest market in the world, that of China and North-East Asia. China is going to be a great economic power this century, and we've got to do more business with the Chinese. Potentially, they represent not only buyers of our minerals and primary produce but tourists. Here is our golden opportunity to be significant beneficiaries of the emerging China. It generates about twenty million outbound tourists a year. In 2003, Australia only got 100,000 of those travellers. Provided we have the skills to be able to take advantage of all these developments, Australia is poised to benefit.

Domestically ours is a small market — even adding New Zealand to the mix, you've still only got around 24 million people — so we do have to export. Ideally, we should seek to be part of a bigger market. With the recent addition of further countries, the European Union now represents 450 million people. Our challenge is to use our collective brainpower effectively in order to compete. That is why we need to do more in research and development. Our federal government needs to be more aggressive about education and training, exports, IT, biotech — all these things need to be at the forefront so we can capitalise on the opportunities in a changing world. In order for Australia to develop trade and export opportunities, we must become a smart nation.

In terms of Australia's economic policy, the Hawke–Keating government was one of the most radical governments we have seen; they gave us a real boost. By contrast, the Howard years have not taken us to the next stage of our development. We haven't done it yet, but we badly need to progress to the next stage, which is to develop the knowledge-based industries. The world is changing dramatically; as I've already argued, this is the century of biotechnology. Seize the day!

The present federal government can also do more for our nation in driving export opportunities around the world. The free trade agreements with Thailand and Singapore are great achievements. However, while I support the Australia–United States Free Trade Agreement in principle, the document that emerged is disappointing in parts. Leaving out the sugar industry is inexcusable. Australia was just too weak to fight for this crucial industry. Nevertheless, on balance the agreement with the US is more positive than negative.

My disappointment on exports is that our Prime Minister and key ministers do not lead enough Australian trade delegations to our key markets. In many markets, governments open doors so the private sector can do business. This is what my government does and why I'm the Minister for Trade. Australia needs to dramatically improve its balance of payments position.

The rise of fanaticism

One of the most emotional events I've ever attended in my life was the service conducted at Parliament House in Canberra for the victims of the Bali bombing. It was an event that moved Australians deeply. Simon Crean acquitted himself well and John Howard genuinely rose to the occasion with his speech.

I met a number of the victims, for whom the whole tragic episode was traumatic and difficult. The victims and their families find it impossible to accept the senselessness of it all; and it was a supremely senseless act. We take our peace and stability too much for granted in Australia.

What should our response be to terrorism? Two things: the first is clearly to bring the perpetrators to justice; the second is to do what Bill Clinton has proposed: go into areas that ferment terrorism, and support programs which lift those societies' standards and provide education, and see to it that the people there have life chances. Religious tolerance, economic development and educational opportunities are the answer. People given a chance to reach their full potential are more likely to do positive things rather than negative things. The origins of this sort of massive negativity are usually in some fanatical viewpoint or some serious disadvantage — it's not just the fault of religion per se. Unfortunately those things can't be eliminated overnight, but that's not a reason not to begin.

In recent decades we've seen the rise of religion again as a force in politics or, more correctly, a rise in the misuse of religion in the politics of some countries. It is an abhorrence to me that wars are fought in the name of religion and that religion is used — whether Christianity, Islam, or Judaism — to justify acts of aggression of one kind or another. In the 1980s a much touted thesis argued that we were heading for a 'clash of civilisations'.[1] That is not necessarily the case. I don't believe that religion, in and of itself, is a power for good or bad. Sometimes it is used for evil purposes, sometimes for good. It depends on which country we are talking about and who is using it.

The religious Right has become very prominent in the US over the past thirty years, a phenomenon that didn't really exist in any formal political sense in the '40s and '50s. This grouping has been influencing politics in the US in an unsavoury way. It's always been there, but now Christian Right fanatics have got in to politics so significantly that they fundamentally shape the Republican Party and its policies. This is a big problem for the health of American democracy.

We haven't had that same experience here except perhaps for the emerging Family First Party in the 2004 federal election. Let's see that we keep religion out of politics. I'm a believer in the separation of church and state — one of the fundamentals that was blurred in the appointment of an Anglican archbishop, Peter Hollingworth, to what should be the secular position of Governor-General.

Beyond Australia there are certainly examples in the world where fanaticism — fundamentalism at its worst — is destroying societies. The experience of the Taliban in Afghanistan was a prime example. I know very well that events outside this country can impact on us here and there is no cause for complacency. After the September 11 attack, we had the burning of a mosque in Queensland. I found that incident outrageous, and I went and supported that community. But it turned out to be a one-off act, perpetrated by a lone individual who has now gone to gaol. Although such activities were few, then or since, the government felt it was important to set up a hotline to help anyone who might have been victimised for being perceived to be on the 'wrong side'. In the event, there were less than a dozen calls, and none of them were substantive. I take that as evidence that our tolerant society is still running smoothly.

Looking inwards

Ours is a vibrant, strong, participatory democracy which has incredible strengths and resilience. We were formed out of a dialogue among the community about nationhood. That discussion and the eventual terms that were agreed and became the foundations of Federation, terms described by journalist Paul Kelly and others as the Australian Settlement,[2] stood us in good stead for a long time. We are safe, we are tolerant, we are multicultural, and while there have been periods in our history when we have lurched from the White Australia Policy through to the extremes of One Nation intolerance, we have always managed as a country to have the spirit of the fair go. Putting that another way, we judge people by what is in their heart, not by the colour of their skin or their religion, and we have been all-embracing as a nation.

In 1987 I participated in a political exchange program to Britain and, as part of the then British Airways fares structure, you could also fly into one country in Europe. I organised a trip to fly into Poland to talk to the Solidarity leadership. Tony Koch, senior journalist with the *Courier-Mail*, accompanied me. On the way back, we went from Warsaw to Berlin by train. Of course, in those days, Berlin was divided by the Wall. We were in East Berlin and approaching the West, when an East German police officer or guard got on the train, knelt down to check under our seats — you needed to have been a pygmy to slide underneath — and then checked our passports. Tony Koch — Koch being a German name — had a new passport so they gave him the once-over.

Tony and I had our photo taken in front of the Wall, and it just reminded me of how lucky we are in Australia. Totalitarian regimes have destroyed so many peoples' lives, and our visit to Berlin in 1987 to see the Wall will always remind me of how totalitarianism can make ordinary people's lives almost unbearable.

By contrast, we often take for granted the freedoms that we enjoy in Australia as part of everyday living. Sure, we have our crime and we have our difficulties, but compared to the rest of the world, we are a safe, free, open democracy — and we can drink the water! We have the wonderful, democratic ability to change government. In the course of my involvement in politics, we have gone from a state government made up of a coalition of the Liberal and National Party, to a National Party government, to a Labor Party government, to a Coalition and back to a Labor Party government again. While the elections have been hotly contested, not one drop of blood has been lost during those changes of government, and the same goes for the rest of Australia. There are very few places in the world that can claim that degree of open democracy, where the will of the people is paramount, not just over governments of the day, but over the military and our institutions.

I dearly hope that my children and other young Australians will continue to be vibrant and strong participating members in our democracy, that they will never be sorry, concerned or fearful of being critical of government but, at the same time, they will respect our parliamentary system. The openness of our democracy needs safeguarding and caring for, but we have one of the greatest democracies on Earth and it is worth fighting for.

Vigorous public debate within Australia is crucial in continuing to refresh our system. On our record of constitutional amendments, there is obviously reluctance among Australians to pass referenda, but in that lies also a healthy scepticism about politicians and governments. Sure there are times when I would like to see Australians more positive on certain issues, but I think the balance is not that far off.

A national agenda?

As I have said, what we sorely lack in Australia is a national vision for the future. I would love to see one developed where future possibilities and potentials are fleshed out and also where the limits of government are clarified.

The impulse towards parochialism is understandable, but it must be kept in perspective. Just as my government is trying to equip Queensland for the twenty-first century, we should be trying to do the same for the nation. It's of great concern that the current federal government is not leading in this vital matter. Australia has to shake itself up or our children and grandchildren are simply not going to have our standard of living.

Among a government's myriad roles is that of ensuring that, by and large, people are free to get on with their lives with minimum government interference. The rights to privacy are of enormous importance. I am firmly of the belief that governments should keep out of people's bedrooms. Consenting adults should be able to have, within the law, whatever relationship they like, provided that children are not harmed as a result and that no forms of abuse are involved. In Queensland we recognise same sex couples and de facto relationships. I think we have lost momentum with these things nationally, however, and old prejudices are creeping back in here and there, hence the debate about abortion which began in November 2004 not long after the federal election. Surely it's a woman's right to choose!

As well as being vigilant about and reducing discrimination, the important element that I want to see cemented into place for Australia's future is one that I have referred to a great deal throughout this book, and that is education — a better education for all. Let's embrace the fact that people learn in different ways and apply more imagination to education; let's view learning as a life-long experience, one that never stops, and let's start it earlier than we currently do. Let's try to understand our past and to learn from it. A smart nation is one that tries to educate all its people for a better economic future, and provides the young especially with a broad education in values, history and humanity. Let's help them realise that sometimes life is not black and white, and that often there are shades of grey. In other words, let's respect the right of others to have a different view. That's what makes it possible for us to all live side by side.

But ultimately whatever we, as an older generation, might try to do for younger people, a lot of the social and political and economic organisation is going to be down to them, their choices and efforts. Power still resides in individuals' hands. My advice to young Australians is to get involved in political and social activity of some kind. Join a party, use your vote intelligently, write to your MP. Be informed and be active. Don't despair when you see all that is going on in your own society and around the world. If enough young people choose this kind of activity, they can and will make a difference.

Towards a republic

Think of Australia as a painting or a work of art, which in many ways it is. While much of it looks right, there are times when I would like to see Australians adding something more to the picture. One of the fundamental things missing is a really mature set of constitutional arrangements. We have a workable enough constitution but it's not the best it can be. I am convinced Australia will not truly find its real place in the world until it's a republic. And I also think those of us who want a republic — and let's keep ourselves broad-based — have to get our act together. The movement for a republic in Australia has to wake up to reality and develop a mechanism to work up some models that we can confidently put to the people. Until that happens we're wasting our time.

Let's have a two-stage process. One, do you want a republic? Two, here are the models. If the vote for a 'republic' is yes, then go out and put up the models and get agreement on the terms of each. And after that, we have a referendum and ask the people to vote on which one they want.

Many of the models floated in Canberra at the Constitutional Convention in 1998 were hopeless and drafted more to satisfy egos than for Australia's benefit. There are basically only two useful approaches: do Australians want the direct election for president, as in the Irish model, or do we want the Governor-General simply appointed a president by federal parliament? In both cases the president would have exactly the same powers as the current Governor-General.

We will always get some academic or lawyer who will produce a clever analysis that says if you put something like this to voters then a shoe could get elected. But I don't believe our constitution should be a product of academics or lawyers alone, or be at their mercy either (and remember, I'm a lawyer). Australia's constitution has got to be worked out by the people themselves with a range of inputs and counsel.

Cultural strength

Beyond our democratic system, what are our other advantages as a nation? Without question it's our culture. Culture is the strength of the community in which you live. It includes all the social norms but it's also the art, the music, the literature. Culture is the way people live, as well as the artistic interpretation of that life. And arts and literature can not only help improve awareness in the culture and how people live, they can change how they live, contributing to enlightenment and to building a better, safer and happier community.

In Queensland we've established the Premier's Literary Awards to encourage writing. The Awards are open to everyone in Australia, and they're also the richest collection of writing prizes in the country. That some of the works deemed worthy of awards may hold possible criticisms of my government doesn't bother me one iota. Artistic expressions are another contribution to the debate and we shouldn't be afraid of debate, nor of criticism. This is illustrative of a new Queensland and why there is a revolution going on here, but it's also emblematic of Australia at large.

It's increasingly difficult to define a 'typical Australian' now. It's not just the variety of food available to us that makes this such a rich society, but the mix of food, writing and art, the mix of ideas, peoples and cultures. Not only are we a melting pot, we've managed that melting pot better, I believe, than anywhere else in the world — certainly a lot better than the Americans have. If you were to ask me what is my personal culture, I would respond that it's made up of numerous elements — as a result of reading widely; of listening to music (my taste in music runs from hard rock through to classical, and I don't even mind a bit of jazz, though it's not my first choice); of a cultural inheritance that includes British strands, as well as Indigenous and multicultural ones. The diversity of Australia has, if you like, educated and formed me as much as anything else.

This multiculturalism is one of the most important aspects of Australia as a 'work in progress'. We should continue to respect and nurture it. And it's built on a terrific early foundation of our society — the sense of egalitarianism, the 'fair go' for all. Australians have traditionally been a warm people, an open people, and that's why we're so well respected in the world; that's why the world likes us. The only frustration I have about Australia is that there are some who always seem to want to turn the clock back or stagnate. To stagnate is to eventually die as a culture.

A PERSONAL FUTURE

Confessions of a perfectionist

Ever since I can remember, I've always wanted to be out there doing something and doing it to the best of my ability; I possess what used to be known as a Type A personality. The word frantic best describes my work ethic. My chief insecurity at any given moment centres around my desire to do a good job. In order not to fall on my face, I tend to give work my full attention, twenty-four hours a day, seven days a week, and to strive as hard as I can.

Like anyone, I've made mistakes and yes, I do agonise over those. Being in this position of premier is a great honour and I don't want to muck it up. To guard against making too many blunders, I rethink my decisions before committing, and try to get it right first time.

Listening to the views of others

Obsessive as I might be about trying to get my decisions right, I still need and appreciate having people around me who tell it like it is; 'yes' people aren't my style.

It seems to me that if you get fifty to sixty per cent of your decisions right, you've done brilliantly. But no one's brilliant enough to do that alone, all out of their own head. You need alternative viewpoints to do this job properly. Ultimately, I make my own mind up but first I will always listen to what others say.

For me, an important source of support resides outside the conventional political environment. Our Community Cabinets, where we go out and people talk to us, I find truly inspirational. The wisdom that may be found among ordinary Australians — more often than not they are extraordinary people when you hear their stories — is always a shot in the arm. People outside the game of politics, those who don't have any vested interests in a matter, can often offer terrific insights. Politicians, governments, political parties and bureaucracies are not the font of all wisdom. On the contrary, such institutions sometimes develop an inward-looking culture, a defensive position. They don't have all the right answers.

To be effective and productive politically, you've got to listen and listen hard to what the people are saying. If you don't, you will never deliver good policies; and if you don't deliver good policies, your political life will be 'short, nasty and brutish'.

Succession planning

Politicians are granted only a certain time, and I've had more than most. During my years in politics, numerous colleagues have been and gone, and I'm still here. That list includes Wayne Goss; Jim Soorley, the former lord mayor; and key ministers, Jim Elder, Keith De Lacey, Anne Warner, David Hamill, Pat Comben, Wendy Edmond, Matt Foley, Steve Bredhauer, Paul Braddy and Bob Gibbs, among others. Clearly, having to be patient for my chance to be premier did me no harm; perhaps it was even 'character-building' as they say. It's been a wonderful experience and I've also been lucky. Of the twenty-six Labor leaders in Queensland's history, I'm now the second longest-serving.

One of my present jobs is to identify and nurture people who can take over and add their bit. Luckily within the Labor Party there are many highly talented individuals — Anna Bligh, Paul Lucas and Rod Welford, just to mention three. I have a strategy to groom them and give them experience, because I never want the Party to go through what happened in the post-Goss era, where we went into Opposition and then had to build almost from scratch. Fortunately, we retained some of the experience of the Goss incumbency, but it's far better for leaders to try to hand over to a successor while still in office.

Top of my agenda, as I have stressed throughout this book, is Smart State. When that is deeply rooted and cemented in the

Queensland psyche and it has changed the state for the better forever, then I will go. If the electorate allows me, I'll hand over to others and do it in a way which is good for Queensland. Ultimately, though, if the people decide your time's up, you're out the door. Nevertheless, it'd be great to leave on a high note — at a time of my choosing and with some degree of dignity and goodwill. To me, leaving well is important.

My intention is to make a clean cut, not to lurk about. With me out, the Labor Party can and will continue to renew itself, as it has done for more than a hundred years.

No lasting regrets

Would I do anything differently if I had my time over again? Other than trying to start Smart State earlier than we did, the answer to that question is no. As the French say, you can't make an omelette without breaking eggs; in order to learn how to do the job of premier, inevitably I had to make mistakes. When I did, I tried to admit them and correct them. The reality is I've been bruised many times along the way but I have learned what people wanted. And you've got to continue learning. So we fine-tune as we go along.

Now I'm better informed than I was when I first became premier and, having been metaphorically kicked in the head for over nine years as ALP leader and seven as Premier, I'm probably a better person, too. Certainly, I believe I've become a more tolerant person than I was in my younger days. In my youth I may have taken a dislike to some people on the basis of their political views. Now I take it as a challenge to try to turn them around if I can and live with them if I can't. I have come to appreciate that every human being on this planet has something to contribute.

What I'll take with me when I go

Two fundamental truths will stay with me. One is that being in public office is a privilege and not a right, and secondly that government is only about getting things done and governing on behalf of the people. It amazes me how easily individuals in positions of power, whether in government or the public service, lose sight of these facts and, while doing so, get caught up in the trappings of power, or go down blind alleys, or lose track of what it is they have been put there to do. The years of Bjelke-Petersen government were sadly full of such examples.

Elected representatives have a position of trust, just like many others in the community who serve — teachers, doctors, nurses, social workers and so on. If I've learned anything through my years in public life it's that trust has to be maintained at all costs.

Getting things done not only requires achieving the trust of voters in the first place, it also requires constant consultation and communication. It means being honest with ourselves as a government, and 'fessing up publicly when we have made mistakes. Various initiatives have been taken to formalise and institutionalise accountability in Queensland through this period — and they have made for a more honest and open government and administration. I staked my claim to the premiership on this new style of politics and government, and was gratified that it struck such a chord with the electorate. Voters clearly know what counts.

I also subscribe to the old but still useful axiom that knowledge is power. Knowledge provides the power to change things for the better. This holds first and foremost for the individual person, but it also holds right up through the social system and at every level, from the smallest units and forms to the government itself. Throughout my time as premier, I have tried to keep learning on the job so that I can do it better and therefore be of greater use to the community; I have at the same time tried to keep focusing on the development of practical policies and encouraging those around me to keep making their contribution. The minute we stop doing this and begin resting on our laurels is the minute we will have served our purpose as a government. I don't believe that time is near just yet — for me, or my team.

What I won't miss

When I do leave politics, it will be wonderful to no longer have to front the media daily. To me, talking to the media is a means to an end. It has been my practice to hold regular media conferences to announce initiatives and make myself available and accountable to Queenslanders through the media. In opting to tell the media about the warts and wrinkles as well as the good news, I have sometimes reduced my media advisers to quivering wrecks. So be it.

It was David Watson, a recent Liberal leader, who first branded me a 'media tart'. At my next media conference, reporters sought my response to the term. I told them that if being a media tart meant that I wanted to get all the government's initiatives into the media, then I pleaded guilty because that's what all politicians want. From then on, of course, I was labelled a self-confessed media tart. Rest assured, I don't want to be on radio or television. My media 'performances' have only ever been a vehicle for me to sell policies or push a point of view rather than just get some kind of fix. Media exposure is just one of the means of achieving all the things I believed in when I was a little kid with my grandmother. Media coverage is a very fickle thing and it lost its magic for me years ago.

The media is a mixed bag. We've heard all the gripes before — the problems of media opting for the superficial over in-depth analysis; skimping on research; zeroing in on the fight and ignoring the message. We politicians have to be careful not to feed the problem. I'll always be grateful to Steve Bishop, my press secretary of almost ten years, for convincing me to throttle back from my former habit of ranting and raving. Television is an honesty barometer. If you get exposure and people see you put the argument with passion and conviction, they pick up on it. They can read you; they see past the distractions. Television is very much like taking truth serum. Still, I have enjoyed a good working relationship with the media and I thank them for that.

Beliefs and personal code

Previously I talked about my childhood, of being immersed in the down-to-earth values of 1950s Australia. My generation — and subsequent generations, too — was also greatly influenced by the ideals of the '60s — the openness, the tolerance, the liberal and even libertarian views that were expounded back then.

Applying Buddhist principles helps a lot of Western people. It is a selfless religion. And you can understand how people can find some peace if they can get rid of some of the mental rubbish they carry around. While I think that some of the principles of Buddhism are excellent in themselves, personally I try to follow Christian principles. To turn the other cheek, to offer forgiveness — such precepts are timeless and ever useful. My children have all been confirmed. Whatever cynicism one may have about organised religions, the principles on which they are based are good.

There is an adaptation of an Eastern precept that works for me, one I've tried to adopt. It's Japanese in origin, I believe, and it goes something like this: The most effective way to annoy your enemies is to be successful. In politics, people regularly want to do you in and sometimes you're tempted to strike back. Instead, it is better get on with it, do positive works and don't take things personally.

On a day-to-day basis, I try to turn the page on bad feelings. I try not to carry grudges — anger is a wasted emotion. Of course I can get angry but it passes. Generally, I try not to waste energy on negative things. I've seen too many people eat their hearts out, destroy themselves with negativity and not be able to let go. When I heard Bill Clinton speaking so powerfully about the situation in the Middle East, his words reinforced that belief for me. Just as it is crucial for those involved in the vexed relationship between Israel and Palestine to let go of negativity, if someone wants to do better and be happier, they've got to personally let go of nonsense and bitterness and anger. The Beatles song 'Let It Be' represents a truly great philosophy, one I try to live by.

It may be a tired old cliché to some, but if you're looking for peace, in the end you've got to find it in yourself. If you're looking for happiness and fulfilment and development, you've got to find it in yourself. To some extent that may be at odds with our Western values, which are so often adversarial or competitive, but you can aim to strike a balance. You can go out and achieve your best by being positive, constructive and working with people without trying to destroy others along the way, without being angry. That is my personal philosophy.

We're all products of our historical period and circumstances, and if you can be successful within the terms of your own inheritance, that's all you can ask for. You should never seek to leave a legacy that's beyond your time or try to aim for posterity. Not only will there always be someone better than you, but we cannot predict the circumstances of the future with any certainty. We should just try to create the brightest possible future that we can.

The next job

As for future roles for myself, I have no fixed plans. The idea of pursuing aid work with the UN appeals to me, as does possible involvement with industries like biotechnology, IT, venture capital, aviation or tourism. One thing is for certain — whatever I do, it will definitely not be political.

Although people in the Party and community have suggested to me, 'Look, why don't you think about going federal? Why don't you put your hat in the ring?' and so forth, notwithstanding my little rush of blood to the head after the 2004 federal election, I'm not interested. I had my run for a federal seat in 1980, and that was to achieve a very specific goal; I wasn't seriously planning to commute to Canberra. If I had wanted to pursue a federal career I would have done that many years ago.

Admittedly, I was interested in federal politics at one stage, and I was approached. Ken Hayward, a Goss government health minister in the 1980s, suggested I run for the federal seat of Fisher. I declined. Michael Lavarch later ran for it and won, then became the federal Attorney-General in the Keating government. That's all water under the bridge. Honestly, I have no regrets; I couldn't be happier with the opportunities I've had. My priority has always been the state of Queensland.

Looking forward

Of the numerous personal tasks to be attended to once I leave office, a top priority will be working on my health and fitness. My mother died at thirty-eight of a complicated heart condition, and her sister died around the age of fifty-two, so my worry is that healthwise my genetic inheritance isn't great.

Most of us Beatties have a never-ending battle with weight issues. (An exception is my sister, Joan, who seems to have managed to keep herself trim and fit all her life, although she does exercise an enormous amount.) Thankfully, my children and my dear wife don't share my problem; if I as much as walk into a fish and chip shop, I reckon my waistline expands. For most of my adult life I have been overweight — sometimes slightly, sometimes significantly. Finally, over the past few years, I have got it under some degree of control. Had I not been able to do so, I would have considered quitting politics. But I could still be another five to ten kilograms lighter. It is a fight every single day.

One difficulty is that I do love food. I am not a big drinker, although occasionally I enjoy a glass of red wine; I am told that it is healthy for middle-aged males with a slight tendency to be overweight to drink good red wine in moderation.

Compounding my problem, wherever I go as premier, whether I am in the bush being offered the best pumpkin scones on the planet or whether I am in the city, the food on offer is always fantastic. I find it hard to say no.

My stint as health minister in the Goss government straightened out my thinking to some extent. It became crystal clear to me that prevention is better than a cure. I have certainly modified my lifestyle as a result. I exercise every morning without fail, dragging my poor old dog Rusty up and down a hill near my home; it would really have to be a bloody hailstorm to stop me. If your mum dies at thirty-eight, it's hard not have some anxiety about your own mortality above and beyond the normal. So I'm strongly motivated to try to live as healthily as I possibly can, to get regular exercise and to keep an eye on my cardiovascular health. And every year I do go and have a health check.

My post-politics wish-list is pretty long. Not only do I intend to sort out my weight problem, I also plan to hone my computer skills, and I'd like to spend a lot of time reading. Learning Italian is another goal. Heather learned German and I did French at school and, while I'm quite hopeless at languages, we are both keen to learn Italian.

Along with my wife, I hanker for some recreation and some peaceful moments in some of our favourite places, both here and overseas. Greece is one of these. We both love the port of Kalamata, a lovely location at the south of the Peloponnese and famous for its olives. We first went there many years ago — BC, before children. I look forward to sitting in this wonderful little fishing village having a meal without anyone there knowing who we are, just being ordinary people — which is what we are, after all. Parts of Italy also draw me back, and I'm keen to explore areas in the south of France, including the caves.

Beautiful, quiet places attract me. Special places that allow you to be reflective. You've got to look at your soul from time to time to know who you are. Currently in our lives that's extremely difficult to do. If you're always in some sort struggle or conflict or policy development or whatever, then opportunities to devote your attention for any length of time are elusive, which is a shame.

We'll also spend time at our favourite haunts in Queensland. It is indeed a long list! One trip we will certainly make is the drive along that wonderful stretch between Brisbane and Sydney, then Sydney to Adelaide via Melbourne. We've spent a reasonable amount of time in Tasmania but we are keen to go back and have another look. We're also itching to do the Indian–Pacific train trip across the continent, Sydney to Perth.

Travelling with Heather, spending time together where people don't know who I am, these are the kinds of things I am anticipating, and I'm positive I will love every minute of it. I am looking forward to being just another person, where what I say or do doesn't matter any more.

I plan to do some cooking, and I also intend to spend some time just wandering around, going to interesting places and trying my hand at new things. Most of all, I look forward to sharing more time with my beloved Heather.

Heather and me

Heather is an amazingly resilient person. Ever since I became involved in the Reform Movement — which was followed by my time as a union secretary, then as Party secretary, and then as humble member and so on, throughout all the highs and lows (and there have been a good many lows) Heather has been at my side. She's suffered through an awful lot. There is no doubt that Heather has had more than enough of politics, yet she knows that there is a contribution we can make, and it is not yet complete.

Once I have retired, it will truly be Heather's time to set our agenda as a couple, and well it should be, too, after the sacrifices she has made.

Frankly, being Premier is the best job I've ever had, and I am not intending to give it up just yet. And Heather is fairly new in her current job, working as an associate professor at the University of Queensland. In other words, for the time being both of us are committed to what we're doing.

When I do leave politics, I want to leave knowing that while I was there I did my best and made things better for people at least to some extent, allowing for the mistakes I've made as any human being would. I have no desire to be a 'somebody'; I've seen too many people destroyed by empty ambition.

Sometimes when Heather and I stroll down to our local coffee shop on a Saturday morning, wearing our daggy old walking clothes, I notice the occasional passer-by looking stunned to see us. I have never bought the hype that some want to attach to my role and my title, especially not when Heather and I consider ourselves to be normal people. Deep down, Heather and I are still a pair of country kids who value things like respect and dignity. We still pinch ourselves that we've been able to get to where we are. And we've never forgotten where we came from.

At the end of all this we know who we are as people. And that's why I both love the job and am so relaxed about one day letting it go. After all, when Peter Beattie goes home for the final time from the premier's office, he will still be a dad with a wonderful partner and kids. I'm really looking forward to that day.

EPILOGUE

To turn ideas into reality in politics requires tremendous application. The movement to reform the Queensland Labor Party began in December 1977, and the final result was Wayne Goss winning government in December 1989 — so it took twelve years to revitalise the Party. The real resurgence of the Party, when it truly came to be seen that ours was the natural party of government in Queensland, had to wait until 1998.

As one of the many individuals who contributed to that process, I found the work hard yet at times exciting. Allowing for setbacks along the way, we had the sense that we were moving forward. Today we see the flowering of the seeds we sowed, the work we have done through the last twenty-eight years.

I would do it all again. The Queensland ALP has been my life. It is a source of enormous personal pleasure to look back over our years in government since 1989, to see how the Labor Party has matured. We've become a party of government. That doesn't mean we take anything for granted — we don't. But Queensland's become a totally different place. It stands tall and it's open; there's a sense of us seeing who we are and what we have here in this state and valuing it all more than ever before. Years ago, if you came here from Sydney or Melbourne, you'd feel like you were in another country. It's not that way any more.

People wonder what attracts a person to politics. As I've said, in my case it boils down to wanting a better education system and wanting to do something about health services, and I also had a strong commitment to social justice and material justice. The only way to effect change in society, as far as I could see, was through political action. Politics is about people, particularly about people from lower socio-economic groups getting a fair go. Australians' commitment to the 'fair go' is, in a sense, our own form of social justice in operation. We don't like tall poppies, we prefer the underdog. We are about allowing everyone a chance to develop themselves so that they might achieve a decent and satisfying standard of living and way of life. That's what a fair go means. The Labor Party is the one true party that works to pull the blocks and impediments out of the way of that fair go for people. But it can't do that from Opposition.

I sincerely believe that Australians are committed to this concept of social justice. You judge somebody by what's in their heart; you don't look at the colour of their skin or their religion or their ethnic origin. Queenslanders are like any other Australians; in the end, they will judge people on how they behave. They believe in the concept of a fair go. That's why in Queensland we have brought in some of the most tolerance-promoting anti-discrimination legislation in Australia. I will continue to promote equal opportunity and moral justice, to end discrimination based on the background of an individual or group.

If you create an environment of openness, one in which innovation is rewarded, and you respect civil liberties, the end result is a tolerant, creative society that prospers and grows. That kind of society produces a strong community, one where there is respect for people's right to be different and to have a different view. In some places in the world, they shoot people who disagree with the authoritarian norms.

Experiencing a difficult start in life spurred my desire to make changes. My commitment to the Smart State program for Queensland, and education generally, reflects what I know about education — that it was and is a great equaliser. Ours is a society where you can come from the most humble of circumstances and you can achieve whatever you want through education and hard work.

I passionately believe education can make the biggest single difference in a person's life. It has the greatest potential to pull you up into a better life, particularly as in Australia there are no old-style structural or class barriers to acquiring an education. And I say this while perfectly aware that fewer than 15 per cent of people who come from my circumstances ever go to university[1] and knowing also that there are other pressures, social pressures, that operate against people in lower socio-economic groups. The point I will always stress is that Australia provides a chance, and in many other countries that chance does not exist. We have to nurture our culture and society so that opportunity exists not only for our generation but for those to come.

ACKNOWLEDGMENTS

Without the support of my long suffering wife, Heather, and our children Larissa, Denis and Matthew, this book would not have happened. They know how very much I love and appreciate them.

Many friends and colleagues have encouraged and assisted me on this book, including Professor Glyn Davis, Manfred Cross, Madeleine McPherson, Steve Bishop, Rob Whiddon, Vicki Nicholls and John Cokley.

I also want to pay special tribute to my late grandmother Mrs Annie Esbensen, who gave me my start in life. Without her none of this would have been possible.

NOTES

Chapter Four: Becoming Absorbed in Politics

1 *Gough Whitlam: In His Own Words*, television program, SBS Television, 10 November 2002

Chapter Five: Agitating for Change, 1977–81

1 Peter Beattie, *In the Arena*, Boolarong Publications, 1990, p. 14
2 See D. J. Murphy, *T. J. Ryan: A Political Biography*, University of Queensland Press, St Lucia, Queensland, 1975
3 Peter Beattie, *In the Arena*, p. 18
4 Bill Hayden, *Hayden: An Autobiography*, Angus & Robertson, Sydney, 1996, p. 330

Chapter Seven: Queensland Before and After Fitzgerald

1 Ross Fitzgerald, *'Red Ted': The Life of E. G. Theodore*, University of Queensland Press, St Lucia, Queensland, 1994, p. 59
2 D. J. Murphy, 'Labor in Power', in D. J. Murphy, R. B. Joyce & Colin A. Hughes (editors), *Labor in Power: The Labor Party and Governments in Queensland, 1915–57*, University of Queensland Press, St Lucia, Queensland, 1980
3 'The Moonlight State', *Four Corners*, television program, ABC TV, 11 May 1987
4 Queensland, Commission of Inquiry into Possible Illegal Activities and Associated Police Misconduct, Fitzgerald Report, Commission of Inquiry into Possible Illegal Activities and Associated Police Misconduct, Brisbane, 1989
5 Fitzgerald Report, p. 200
6 For example, Queensland, Criminal Justice Commission, *Integrity in the Queensland Police Service: Implementation and Impact of the Fitzgerald Inquiry Reforms*, Criminal Justice Commission, Brisbane, 1997; Queensland, Criminal Justice Commission, *Police and Drugs: A Follow-up Report*, Criminal Justice Commission, Toowong, 1999

Chapter Eight: Learning the Ropes, 1987–89

1 Peter Beattie, *In the Arena*, pp. 104–5
2 ibid., pp. 132–37

Chapter Ten: The Road to Premier, 1996–98

1 Peter Beattie (Leader of the Opposition), *Borbidge institutes 62 reviews in 70 days*, media release, 26 April 1996
2 Peter Beattie (Leader of the Opposition), media release, 22 March 1996, referring to CJC Media Release of 21 March 1996
3 David Smith, 'Crime Claim', *Gold Coast Bulletin*, 27 August 1996
4 Hansard, Queensland Legislative Assembly, 'No Confidence in Attorney-General and Minister for Justice', 20 August 1997, pp. 3065–75
5 Peter Beattie, Opening Address, State Conference of the Australian Labor Party (Queensland Branch), 8 June 1996
6 Ross Fitzgerald, 'Beattie Coup Draws Party Together', *Courier-Mail*, 13 June 1996
7 Campaign 98 Queensland Labor, 'Job Security for Queensland Workers'
8 Mike Kaiser (ALP campaign director), *Labor directs that preferences will go to One Nation last*, media release, 26 May 1998

Chapter Eleven: In Government, 1988 and Beyond

1 Anna Bligh (Minister for Families, Youth and Community Care/Disability Services), *Historic day for child protection in Queensland*, media release, 25 March 1999
2 M. Franklin & S. Parnell, 'State Seeks Inquiry on Electoral Rorts Claims', *Courier-Mail*, 16 August 2000, p. 4
3 ibid.
4 Damien Murphy, 'Independents Muddy the Political Waters up North', *Courier-Mail*, 27 January 2001
5 Peter Beattie (Premier and Trade), *Beattie poised to fully fund $150M package to stop tree clearing*, media release 18 January 2004
6 Peter Beattie (Premier and Trade), *New office will manage growth in booming SEQ*, media release, 28 January 2004

Chapter Twelve: Learning From Others

1 Paul Reynolds, *Lock, Stock and Barrel: The Political Biography of Mike Ahern*, University of Queensland Press, St Lucia, Queensland, 2002

2   Hansard, Queensland Legislative Assembly, Peter Beattie, 'Terrorism, United
    States', ministerial statement, 12 September 2001, pp. 2623–24

Chapter Thirteen: Families and Security

1   Hansard, Queensland Legislative Assembly, Peter Beattie, 'Howard
    Government; Income Inequality', ministerial statement, 12 November 2003,
    p. 4789, referring to Peter Saunders, 'Examining Recent Changes in
    Income Distribution in Australia', Social Policy Research Centre,
    University of New South Wales, Sydney, October 2003,
    <http://www.sprc.unsw.edu.au/dp/DP130.pdf>
2   ibid.
3   Queensland Police Service, *Statistical Review 2003–04*, Brisbane, Queensland,
    2004, <http://www.police.qld.gov.au/pr/services/statsnet/0304/03_04.shtml>

Chapter Fourteen: Indigenous Australia

1   Queensland, Department of the Premier and Cabinet, *Cape York Justice Study*,
    report prepared by Tony Fitzgerald for the Department of the Premier and
    Cabinet, Brisbane, 2001, p. 56, <http://www.communities.qld.gov.au/
    community/publications/capeyork.html>
2   Hansard, Queensland Legislative Assembly, Peter Beattie, 'Indigenous
    Communities, Cape York', ministerial statement, 18 March 2004, p. 37

Chapter Seventeen: Australia

1   Samuel Huntington, *The Clash of Civilizations and the Remaking of World
    Order*, Simon & Schuster, New York, 1996
2   Paul Kelly, *100 Years: The Australian Story*, Allen & Unwin, Sydney, 2001

Epilogue

1   Richard James, 'Socioeconomic Background and Higher Education
    Participation', Centre for the Study of Higher Education, University of
    Melbourne, April 2002, Table 2.1., p. 6, <http://www.dest.gov.au/archive/
    highered/eippubs/eip02_5/eip02_5.pd>

INDEX